Living For Higher Purpose

Story of a City Boy Who Survived the Viet Nam War
by Living for Jesus and Others

Reverend Peter G. Vu

To

Thank you for your support. May this book
give you a different viewpoint of the Viet Nam
War & lift you up in your most difficult moments.
☺ Fr. Peter

First published by Dog Ear Publishing
4011 Vincennes Rd
Indianapolis, IN 46268
www.dogearpublishing.net

ISBN: 978-1-4575-5816-0

This book is printed on acid-free paper.

Printed in the United States of America

I dedicate this book to the following people:

- My loving and faithful God and God's son Jesus, who has always been by my side to protect, support, comfort, and show me the way.
- My family and ancestors: Great-grandparents, grandparents, parents, uncles, and aunts, who have never wavered in their support for me and have continued to protect and cheer for me beyond this life.
- My friends and benefactors: These kind and generous people are like my guardian angels, who God has sent to me throughout my life to give me a helping hand in times of need.

I'm forever grateful to my God and indebted to all of you. May our loving and faithful God repay you abundantly and continue to bless you and your loved ones.

Table of Contents

Introduction

The Viet Nam War, like other wars in human history, has entered the American consciousness and remained a bewilderment for the present and future generations to discern and wonder. This war divided America, Viet Nam, the public at large, and many families. It brought tears, bloodshed, suffering, hatred, anger, chaos, loss, and destruction to all involved. Many books have been written and movies have been made to reflect various viewpoints and opinions. But, few books have been written from the perspective of a witness and survivor of this war. Viet—the main character of this memoir—witnessed the end of the War and lived through the horrible days under a Communist regime.

During this war, people lined up on both sides to support it and protest it. After the war ended, no one seemed to care about its victims or wanted to speak up for them and come to their aid. Viet wants the world to know what happened to its victims and what was left behind after everyone left the country. He survived the aftermath and escaped by boat to search for freedom and a new life beyond his broken homeland. He spent about a week at sea fighting for his life against hunger, thirst, heat, seasickness, waves, violent storms, sharks, Communists and their allies, pirates, the idea of cannibalism, and death. Thankfully, by God's grace and with the help of some good people from a South Korean ship, Viet was rescued along with his boat mates and dropped off at a refugee camp in Singapore. After several months at this camp, his father sponsored him to come to America.

Viet struggled to learn English and adapt to the new culture in America. He battled loneliness, hopelessness, discrimination, lack of resources, and other issues that a refugee endures in a new land. He also tried to discern the priesthood vocation and decided to follow his Lord's footsteps and serve His Church. With this, he left behind numerous great opportunities of the Promised Land and entered the seminary. He conquered many challenges of seminary life and acquired new skills and disciplines to help him become an effective priest for God's people. After ten years of seminary training, Viet was ordained a priest for the Diocese of Grand Rapids, Michigan. He has been a faithful and loving priest for 20 years and is looking forward to serving Christ's church for many more years.

Viet has shared a little bit of his life story in his Sunday homilies and other workshops in the last 20 years. His friends and parishioners have urged him to write this book so that they will have a full picture of his amazing life. This book is partly a history book and partly a personal diary. As the two parts of this story weave together, one will see the divine presence and the secrets of life that have helped Viet survive throughout his life. He relied on the protection of his ancestors and the help of Guardian Angels—kind and generous people—that God sent him along the way. Most important, he has looked up to his loving God and a higher purpose to stay alive and move forward each day.

Hence, Viet's memoir has taken the title *Living for a Higher Purpose*. This book will guide readers through many stories of Viet's life and eventually help them determine what that higher purpose is. It also discusses many popular, current issues such as war and its victims, refugees and their life's challenges, life under a Communist regime, core curriculum, how the world views America, the relationship between Catholicism (Christianity) and Buddhism, and much more.

After reflecting on various issues and discerning life from different viewpoints, Viet will help readers come to the same conclusion about the secret of a fulfilling and joyful life. That is, a person should use his or her life to serve Jesus and other people. By sticking to this way of living, a person will find meaning and unending joy even in the dark night of his or her soul. This person will always trust in God's love on the Cross of Jesus to guide, protect, strengthen, and encourage him or her throughout his or her life. My hope is that you will find comfort, joy, hope, and answers for your life issues by journeying through this memoir with Viet. May God's love always be before you, beside you, and behind you all the days of your life.

Fr. Peter G. Vu

Living For Higher Purpose

Story of a City Boy Who Survived the Viet Nam War
by Living for Jesus and Others

Reverend Peter G. Vu

Chapter 1:

Searching for Life and Salvation
on the Days of Apocalypse

"One, two, three," a boy facing a wall with his eyes closed keeps counting. His friends scatter looking for a place to hide in the neighborhood where they grew up together and knew everyone so well. There are occasional giggles and whisperings as this group of kids tries to keep themselves well hidden from the counting boy, who seems oblivious to all the fun his friends are enjoying. His voice seems to pick up with a faster pace as he says, "…seventeen, eighteen, nineteen." A few slackers speed up with their search for the best hiding places, but change their minds at the last minute and decide to go home to hide instead. That is probably the best hiding place of all. Even the most seasoned detective cannot find them there.

After several minutes of counting that seem to go on forever and commotion from kids looking for the best hiding places, the whole neighborhood is reduced to silence. The boy who counted a moment ago stops abruptly at thirty and calls out at the top of his lungs, "Ready or not, here I come!" When he closed his eyes a moment ago, he could sense all the familiar sounds and smells of the neighborhood. He could tell where all the yelling and screaming was coming from. A couple of his neighbors often talk with their household members at the top of their lungs, as if they were deaf. Street vendors also frequent the neighborhood and call out their selling slogans, letting everyone know what is best about their products. His whole neighborhood is always full of sounds that intertwine with one another to create a magical concert for its residents and visitors. The intoxicating smells of the tropical flowers and fruits make the whole neighborhood feel like the Garden of Eden, where everyone can feel safe and have anything they want.

The counting boy slowly opens his eyes to an eerie silence of a neighborhood that he once thought he knew it quite well. All his friends had gone into hiding, and he now must look for them. He wonders where he can begin his search. Maybe he can find a couple of kids behind the gate of the neighborhood coffee shop. Or perhaps some of them are hiding in the courtyard of the huge palace at the end of the main street leading to the neighborhood. As he walks down the street searching for his friends, he calls out their names and makes all kinds of weird noises, such as shaking the front gates of each house and dragging a stick along the fence to rattle up the fainthearted. He had to get them to come out of their hiding holes! He learned this tactic from watching some Western movies in which the cowboys would herd their cattle by whistling and hollering.

His tactic works as he finds his first victim giggling behind a big coconut tree. After several minutes, he finds and gathers half of his group of friends who play the game with him. He also learns from those he's found that some of the hiders went home. It would certainly be difficult for him to find those friends! He calls them the "MIA or Missing in Action" buds, who often do not complete the game because their parents call them home or they must go take care of something else. After chatting with one another for a little while, the group decides to call it a day. What everyone does not realize is that a couple of kids are still hiding in a secret place within their beloved neighborhood. And yet everyone goes home that day full of contentment, as if they had just completed an amazing project. They are totally oblivious to the couple of their buddies left behind in some hiding hole.

That is the neighborhood where a young boy named Viet grew up. It is a place where everyone knows each other well and the kids play on the streets without a care in the world. Viet used to play soccer, badminton, volleyball, hopscotch, rope jumping, marbles, and other fun games with his neighborhood friends. They all go to Catholic Church and Buddhist Temple together without any concern or question. One of the common activities they enjoy doing together annually is going to Midnight Christmas Mass together and hanging out late afterward. Unlike Christmas in many Western countries, Christmas in Viet Nam is not a national holiday, and all children went to school the next day. In fact, students had to attend school all day the day before and the day of Christmas. The only holidays that students were excused from school were the couple of days for Lunar

New Year. They also had to go to school six days a week and were allowed only Sunday off. Although Viet and his friends must work hard in school, they seem to enjoy the normal life of a kid.

What they do not know is that a horrible war is going on not too far from their seemingly safe neighborhood. That war has been raging for a couple of decades, but most children in Saigon City have not been told much about it. Among the thousands of lives that have been lost, many of them are children. Hundreds of children have been recruited to fight for the northern Communists, while many have been displaced or lost their families and homes.

The safe bubble that Viet and his neighborhood friends have played under for years comes crashing down during several historical days in April. Their whole neighborhood was shelled mercilessly and turned into a war zone. That is the day their beloved city of Saigon falls into the hands of the Communists.

Viet and his friends grew up in a middleclass neighborhood near Saigon city that is about a ten-minute bicycle ride to the main airport in South Viet Nam called Tan Son Nhut. They all live such a sheltered life that they are caught by surprise when Saigon falls and the horrible bombing and shooting takes place around their neighborhood. They have never seen any news about the Viet Nam War. All they do is go to school, play on their neighborhood streets, stop by a church or temple for some prayers, and come home to eat and sleep. They do not watch much television except some traditional shows and occasional Western movies. In fact, most of them do not have their own televisions and usually huddle together in a living room of a wealthy family in their neighborhood to watch their favorite shows. The collapse of Saigon and the invasion of the northern Communists come as a total surprise for Viet and his friends. They thought it was the end of the world.

Viet, who was raised in a Catholic family and listened to the Sunday readings in church from the Book of Revelation cannot believe that he would experience the same vision right there in person. As an avid Bible reader and a regular churchgoer, Viet recalls one of the big topics in that Sacred Book was the last day of the world or the Apocalypse. That is the day that God will bring judgment on our sinful world, wipe it all out, and create a new world. The scene of that historical day is quite chaotic and scary. Wars and famine will break out. Natural disasters such as earthquakes, floods, volcanoes, drought, and so on will occur worldwide. The sun will darken, and the moon and the stars will fall out of the sky. The Sacred Book describes pain and a dark, bleak, and horrifying picture of the last day. In addition, hunger, bloodshed, killing, fighting, and death come in abundance on the last day.

Viet wonders if all the prophecies in the Book of Revelation have finally come true and the last day is finally here. As he looks up to the sky, he sees it filled with military jets and helicopters taking off from the nearby airport. He has never seen that many airplanes on the sky before. Suddenly, some of them are shot down or fly into each other. The accident leaves a trail of black smoke and a buzzing sound of a descending object that meets the horizon with a loud crash.

After watching this scene play out in the sky for several hours, Viet is utterly speechless, but decides to check out one of the main roads leading to downtown Saigon. He wants to see what has happened. The scene is not any better than near his home. He sees tanks, military vehicles, and soldiers running every which way on the road. Some of the soldiers wear complete uniforms and helmets, while others throw away their uniforms and run around only in their undershirts and shorts. None of them carried a gun or weapon. Viet later learned that the soldiers striped away their uniforms because they did not want to get shot. In many cases, they simply walked around with a white flag or their hands up to show the Communists that they surrendered. That busy road to downtown Saigon was also littered with dead corpses, fresh blood, and all sorts of abandoned weapons. He had never seen anything like that on the road before.

Full of horror and complete sadness, Viet turns his eyes to the safe neighborhood where he and his friends played just a couple of days ago. But the neighborhood playground—his cocoon—is now completely deserted. He finds no familiar person wandering around his beloved neighborhood. Like the game of hide and seek that they played recently, most of his neighbors and friends have gone into hiding, trying to keep themselves safe in the most secure places of their homes. Viet begins to wonder why he is still standing out in the open and risking being hit by a stray bullet or bomb. Suddenly, he hears buzzing sounds above his head and some loud explosions near his home. He realizes it is not safe to be in the open, and now it is time for him to seek shelter with his family. His home has no basement or bomb shelter. His family must create a makeshift bunker of large, thick planks of oak wood. Sadly, they later reused those planks to make caskets for Viet's grandparents and great-grandparents.

The bunker is dark, hot, uncomfortable, and ill-ventilated. They must squat and sit knee-to-knee next to each other in the bunker. They also take a break every few hours and go out to stretch and breathe some fresh air. Their electricity and water has been cut off and the entire neighborhood is in darkness. All the local food stores and outdoor markets are closed. Viet's family must ration their stored-up foods and dash to a local well to bring back water. They try to cook some meals over coal, woods, sticks, straws, papers, books, and even paper currency.

Viet remembers these difficult days quite well as he tries to help his family in every way he can. He goes out to his family garden in the back of the house a couple of times a day to pick some vegetables such as squash, pea, herbs, and several Oriental plants for food. He also gives his parents a hand in butchering chicken, ducks, and rabbits that they raise in the back yard to survive through the last days of the Viet Nam War. Unfortunately, the shelling of the nearby airport and the martial law that restricts all movements in the city of Saigon continued for more than a week. Viet can see their food ration beginning to dwindle. Their little garden is picked out to almost nothing. Their poultry is butchered right down to just a couple of chickens. Their bags of rice have mostly been used up, with only one small bag left. He does not know where they will get their food in the coming weeks.

However, Viet has always had a strong faith in God and recalls how God came to the rescue of God's people in their difficult moments of the Old Testament. He remembers how God performed a miracle for the widow of Zarephath and her son and never let her bag of flour and jar of oil go empty. Viet's faith is gradually strengthened and renewed as he spends time in prayer with his family during this challenging period. They help him learn to put on the armor of faith when time get tough and teach him valuable life lessons about survival. In the beginning, he thought he would never be able to make it through the aftermath of a long war like the Viet Nam War. The whole social structure was turned upside down, and there was a lot of destruction. The survivors have very little to live on, but they will have to press on despite the challenges and uncertainty of the time.

During this Apocalypse-like period in Saigon, two incidents stood out distinctly for Viet. They impacted his life and left an indelible mark on his memory about this difficult time. The first incident happened when his family's food ration was about to run dry. They had butchered all their poultry, picked their whole garden, and had nothing left except their family pets. Viet remembers his family had a few dogs and cats, and he knew them quite well. He helped raise and take care of them, such as feeding them, bathing them, and playing with them. He had grown close to one of the family dogs and played with it almost every day. Suddenly, on this particular day, his family had no food left. His family told him to help butcher his beloved dog.

"Viet," his grandpa calls. "Would you please give me a hand? Take the dog, Spotty, to the backyard and wait for me there." This dog was called Spotty because he had dark spots all over his white fur coat.

"What are we going to do with Spotty, grandpa?" asks Viet. "Are we going to give him a nice shampoo bath?"

"No, we're not going to give it any shampoo bath. He looks just fine. But, we'll have to butcher it!" answers his grandpa.

"We're going to do what?" startles Viet. "We can't do that, grandpa." He pauses to process the shocking news. He then pleads, "Can't we butcher something else, grandpa? Spotty has been our family pet for a long time. We can't hurt him like that!" Tears start rolling down his cheeks, and he sobs.

"I know, grandson." His grandpa tries to calm him, but he explains, "It is very tough for me to do that to Spotty too. But, we have no other choice. If we don't butcher him, we'll have nothing to eat and we'll all die of starvation. Do you understand that?"

He then gently pulled Viet close to him and gave him a kiss on his head. Viet reluctantly nodded his head as his eyes welled up with tears. Still, his heart was torn between his loyalty to his family and his love for Spotty. He did not know what to do, and he certainly did not want to disobey his grandpa.

Although he refused to kill his pet, his family insisted that he had to carry it out and help save his family. He had never seen his family or heard of anyone ever eating a dog before. But, he had no choice. He had to butcher his beloved pet to save his family. He led his favorite dog to the backyard of his home where his grandpa was waiting for them. He saw the dog's tail wag feverishly as if it thought something great was about to happen. Perhaps Spotty remembered the times they had taken him back here to feed him or when Viet played catch with him on this same ground. It did not know what was about to happen.

Viet couldn't help but recall the classic bible story about Abraham dragging his beloved son to a mountain to sacrifice him and show his loyalty to God. Fortunately, God could see Abraham's faithfulness and decided to spare his son by giving him a ram for sacrifice instead. But, this time there was no ram or anything else to take Spotty's place.

Viet held down tight on Spotty's four legs while his grandpa butchered it. His hands were trembling and tears rolled down like a flowing river on his cheeks. He prayed and hoped that this nightmare would end soon, but he did not know when that would be. He did not like what happened to his favorite pet and yet he thanked God for the opportunity to be around his grandpa and get to know him a little better.

Viet came to respect his grandpa for the wisdom and guidance and his family in the darkest and most difficult time of their lives. He appreciated the life lessons that his grandpa taught him that day about life survival and tough choices. In real life, we will be presented with many tough choices and difficult decisions. These choices and decisions will make a person cry and tear out his or her heart. But, a wise and decent person will always pick his or her family and its survival before anything else, even if one must sacrifice his or her favorite pet. A person will surely put the interests of the whole, such as his or her family, before his or her own. Since that unforgettable day, Viet looked up to his grandpa and came to him whenever he needed guidance or wanted to know what he had to do in his daily life. Indeed, he found a wonderful source of guidance and survival in his grandpa.

Although the experience in the backyard was sad and terrifying for Viet, he learned many valuable lessons about life survival and sacrifices. In life, sometimes Viet has had to make personal sacrifices, like killing his favorite pet, to achieve something great, such as helping his family survive. Along with that personal sacrifice, Viet learned about the importance of obedience and taking orders. If he did not listen to his grandpa and do what he was asked to do, things in his home would have never gotten done, and his family might have died from starvation. Worse yet, there would have been a big fight and chaos in his family. The greatest life lesson Viet learned is the importance of putting his family or the common good before himself and his interests. After all, without his family, his life would not be worth living. Perhaps that is why our Lord Jesus came down to earth and sacrificed His life on the Cross to keep His family together and bring them life and salvation.

Another incident that stayed with Viet until the day he died took place when he helped cook for his family during the difficult days after the Viet Nam War ended. Apparently, they did not have any fuel for cooking and had to use any material available to make a fire, including burning paper currency. Viet remembers his family handed him a stack of paper currency and told him to go cook dinner with it. He knew that the entire city of Saigon was under a strict curfew when the northern Communists took over, and everything was completely shut down. That meant he could not do anything with all that money in his hands. He knew his family would not want him to keep that stack of money for his college fund or future use. They wanted him to use that money as fuel to cook dinner for them. Perhaps that was the first time he learned that someone could use paper currency literally as fuel material. But, he did not want to waste all that money! Perhaps they might need it in the future. He reluctantly took it to the cooking site.

"Would you please help me get the fire going, Viet?" asked his grandma.

"Sure, grandma," answered Viet. "I'll help you."

"Good. Thank you," said grandma.

"What are we cooking, grandma?" inquired Viet.

"Just the usual. Some rice and some vegetable soup," replied grandma.

"Oh, that sounds delicious. I love that, grandma!" complimented Viet. Then, he made a quick glance of the backyard and found no more wood or anything else to start the fire for cooking.

"Grandma, we have nothing here for fuel," questioned Viet with a voice of concern. "How are we going to start the fire? What are we going to cook with?"

"Grandson, not too worried," grandma reassured him. "I already had that figured out."

"You do, grandma?" inquired Viet. "What is it?"

"We're going to get our fire going with the money you're holding in your hand," replied grandma.

"Are you sure, grandma?" asked Viet in surprise. "But, what are we going to do in the upcoming weeks if we burn all this money?"

"You worry too much, grandson," calmly reassured grandma. "God will take care of us tomorrow and beyond. For the Bible says, 'Let tomorrow take care of itself. For today has troubles of its own.' Namely, let's just worry about today for now." Then, she handed Viet a small stack of money bills in all sorts of denominations.

"Start the fire with all of that money," said grandma. "I hope that'll be enough to cook our rice and soup for today."

"I'll make that work, grandma," replied Viet.

He tried to start the fire with several low-denomination bills as his hands were trembling holding the burning bills. This was the first time he had burned money. He threw in several more bills to get the fire going. He did not know how smoky it was to cook something with money bills or papers. His eyes filled with tears. But, he was not sure if that was because of the smoke or because of the stack of money he had to burn for cooking. He found it difficult to burn the high-denomination bills. Still, he had to burn all the money to cook the whole pot of rice.

On that day, grandma taught Viet many wonderful lessons about life and its survival. He learned to trust God more and not let the challenges of today make him worry too much about tomorrow. For God, our source of life and salvation, will always be here to help us. Burning that money to cook a meal also helped Viet learn to detach himself from money and worldly possessions and put the survival of his family above everything else. He began to look at life as a bigger picture and realized that he should not focus and live for money and worldly things. Rather, he should live and work for a higher purpose, namely, his family. Doing so would add more flavor to his life and make it worth living.

As Viet has matured in his life, he often looked back on this cooking experience and would be grateful for many valuable life lessons it left with him. He learned that money and worldly possessions should not be the purpose of his life. For their values would run out at some point, just like that stack of money in his hands that day. All it was good for was to be used for cooking. Furthermore, money comes and goes. He might have thought it was the end of the world when he saw his family burn all their valuable assets to survive. But, the truth is that provided his family was safe and could survive through these Apocalypse-like days, they would be able to work hard and rebuild that fortune with the help of God. Sometimes, people become too attached to money and worldly possessions, and hence they become selfish and greedy with God's blessings for them. They hold on tightly to those things, and do not want to share those blessings with people around them, especially the poor and the misfortunate. They let worldly things shackle them, take over their lives, and put a value on all their relationships.

What they do not realize is that God gives them all those worldly things to serve God and one another. Instead, they become slaves to worldly things and treat all relationships around them like trash. In the end, all they get is a stack of money without anyone to share it with.

What Viet learned from that cooking experience is totally opposite of what the world often tells us. He learned that what matters the most at the end of the day is the relationships that he could save and maintain. He was proud and honored that he could help save his family's lives and preserve its peace amidst chaos and destruction. That cooking experience forever changed his view of money and worldly possessions and began to shape his life mission.

Throughout human history, there have been all kinds of conflicts and wars. In addition, there have been an endless number of natural and manmade disasters. All these events have created a sense of Apocalypse or the Last Day, pain, suffering, tears, sadness, hunger, death, chaos, uncertainty, hopelessness, and other headaches. Many lives have been displaced, whereas others have lost their lives or faced seemingly unbearable challenges. We wonder where these poor victims could possibly find strength and help move forward from their piles of rubble. Surprisingly, even in those dark and depressing moments, we can still find God's presence and saving power. For wherever there is love, one will be able to find God's saving power.

Surely there was plenty of love in Viet's family. That was enough to warrant God's saving power for them amid the death and destruction of the Viet Nam War. Viet and his family were saved because of their love for each other. That love, along with God's love for them, helped shelter them from the flying bullets and hopeless situation at the end of the Viet Nam War. Through that ordeal, Viet also learned to put his family and love for Jesus above his own life. That gave him the courage and willingness to make many personal sacrifices for his family. He was happy to do anything for his Lord Jesus and family, including laying down his life for them. He simply imitated what his Savior taught him: "There is no greater love than this, one lays down one's life for one's friends" (John 15:13). Love is what saved the day, even the Apocalypse day.

Chapter 2

Searching for Reasons to Live in the Land of the Dead

The love of God and their love for each other were what saved Viet and his family during the days of the Apocalypse. But, that was just the beginning of his long and amazing adventure through life. Viet and his family survived those horrible days at the end of the Viet Nam War. The days of martial law and curfews thankfully came to an end and life was supposedly back to normal. However, it was not quite normal at all. Viet and his countrymen now had to live under the rules and control of the Communists. After defeating the United States-backed regime of South Viet Nam, the Communists of North Viet Nam united the entire country and established a new government in Viet Nam.

The first order of business for the new government was to round up all the personnel of the South Viet Nam regime. Although the Communists harbored anger and revenge against their countrymen in the South who collaborated with the United States, they hid that dark emotion and their wicked intentions in rounding up their former enemies. They established hundreds of reeducation camps around the country, even in Siberia, with Russia carrying out their roundups and detaining men and women of the former regime. They told the public and the world that these men and women had betrayed their country and followed a foreign government like the United States and its corrupted way of life. Now they must repay their debts and sins that they committed against their country by attending the camps for "just a week" and learning about all the wonderful things that Uncle Ho—the Communist leader—would give them. The new government claimed they had misunderstood Communism and Socialism. They needed to be reeducated and enlightened about the new way of life. After they got to know Communism and Socialism better, they would gladly embrace it and see the many wonderful things it would bring to society, families, and individuals. They claimed everyone would have a better life, and their society would be the envy of the world. But, the truth is this: It was all a big lie and Viet would find this out during his twelve years of living under the Communist regime.

Viet was just five years old and had finished first grade when his father, who worked for the South Viet Nam regime in its National Security team, had to leave him and his family for one of those camps under the order of the Communists. They lied to him and all the men and women of the former regime when they said they had to leave their families for only a week. Viet remembers clearly his father's farewell as he waved to him: "I'll be back after a week," he said. "They promised that I'll only have to stay at the camp for a week. So, be good and take care of your mom and sisters." Then, with a big duffle bag on his shoulder, he waved goodbye and hopped on a government-owned bus to be taken to one of the reeducation camps. No one knew to which camp Viet's father was taken. Viet recalled coming into the house with his family that morning feeling completely overwhelming by the responsibilities that he had to undertake as "the man of the house." He also felt as if the sky was caving in and the whole world was turning dark. He did not know what he was going to do in the upcoming days. That was the last time Viet saw his father as a free man until 12 years later when he was released from the reeducation camp.

A week came and went, but Viet's father did not return home. Viet's family began to panic and wondered where they could find him or if they would ever see him again. That was the first lie that Viet's family and many of his countrymen experienced under the Communists and the beginning of a series of lies that they experienced with the new government regime. Viet's mother began to check various contacts and tried to track down where her husband was being held. After many attempts and tearful prayers, she learned where his camp was. She quickly packed food and many necessities to take him. She and Viet set out on a long trip to visit him. After several hours of public busing, during which they had to ride with all kinds of poultry and be packed like sardines, Viet and his mother ended up at a village northwest of Saigon. They encountered some villagers who were dressed in colorful sarong. They looked like some tribal folks in Africa or South America. Viet later learned that those were the mountaineers who collaborated and fought side-by-side with the United States Special Forces during the Viet Nam War.

Viet and his mother approached the camp. It is surrounded by a six-foot-tall bamboo fence with razor-sharp barbed wire and a high security gate flanked by armed guards. They asked the guards about Viet's father. After waiting a long time for them to check for Viet's father, they learned he was not being held there. They had to leave in disappointment, and they dragged home all the food and supplies on another long bus ride. They had to start their search for Viet's father from square one. They spent much money bribing authorities and checked out many government contacts to figure out where Viet's father was being held.

A couple of months later, they found out where his camp was and tried to repack everything to head out to another village, which was more than 50 miles north of the first place they travelled. After an early and long ride on public busing, Viet and his mother came to a village that was far removed from a city or any civilization. Like the last camp, this one was heavily guarded. They had to wait for hours at the gate before the camp director approved their paperwork to see Viet's father. At least they found his camp and were not turned away. They said a prayer to thank God for that miracle. The door to the waiting area was finally opened, and Viet's father came out with a dozen other men to see their families.

Viet's father shook their hands and was thrilled to see them. He looked a bit dark, tired, and skinny. His voice seemed to be rattling, and his eyes were a bit distracted. He shared with Viet and his mother some of the hard labor that the Communists were subjecting him and other prisoners in the last several months. He was afraid that the guards might hear what he said and get him into trouble later. He whispered that he had to cut down trees, break boulders into small pieces, remove ordinances, and so on. His hopeful and trusting spirit in the Communist government on the day of his departure was totally gone. He seemed to be worried about something during their meeting. Perhaps, he wondered who was going to take care of his young family and when he would be released from that hell hole. Maybe he was trying to figure out how he could hide his identity and all the work he did at the National Security Office for the South Vietnamese government.

If there was a group of former regime officials that the Communists would hate the most, it would be folks who worked with the

Intelligence Agency like Viet's father. They thought that these people collaborated with the US Central Intelligence Agency (CIA) and other foreign spy networks to hurt and destroy the Communists from the inside. These "bad" people would be sent to Siberia in Russia or a notorious prison in North Viet Nam like the Hanoi Hilton, where Senator John McCain and many high-value American prisoners of war (POW) were imprisoned. Many would never be seen again.

As their visit continued, many guards were watching them like a hawk to prevent any funny business or prison breakout plan from taking place. Their short visit of half an hour quickly ended, and there were lots of tears. They said farewell to each other and took another long ride on a public bus home to Saigon, not knowing what their future might be.

Since that visit, Viet's father was moved to half a dozen more camps within a period of twelve years. His family continued to visit and bring him food and supplies, especially cigarettes and a few other valuable items to give the camp officials in exchange for lenient treatment. Viet learned that most of the camps in South Viet Nam were used to keep low-ranking prisoners, whereas the ones in the North or in Siberia were for the important or the most hated former officials. He also learned another lie that the Communists said about the reeducation camps. They were not like a regular school or a Boy Scout summer camp in which the Communists would teach the former regime supporters everything they needed to know about Communism and Socialism. Rather, they were more like the new version of the World War II (WWII) concentration camps in Asia. All varieties of inhumane treatment and systematic torture happened in the diabolical camps. The Communists created the reeducation camps partly to extract information from their captives and partly to carry out revenge against their enemies without attracting attention from the International community. Many people condemned the WWII concentration camps, and human rights violations happened at those camps. But they were nowhere to be found when it came to the reeducation camps, even though human rights abuse and bad treatment took place at these camps. Viet felt there is a double standard by the international community in its outcry and defense of prisoners of war when it comes to the victims of the reeducation camps compared to the ones of WWII concentration camps. The world mostly forgot these poor souls after the Viet Nam War. Or, perhaps it felt helpless in securing the release of the prisoners in the reeducation camps.

Perhaps the Communists were smarter than the whole international community when they called the camps reeducation camps instead of the concentration camps. They seemingly outsmarted and fooled the whole world with their propaganda and messaging about their evil work. They carried out bad treatment, torture, and killing at those camps without any condemnation from the world. They learned from history how the world condemned the German Nazis and the Cambodian Khmer Rouge for their evil policies that included mass killing. Indeed, they tried to avoid bad publicity on their regime and evil acts. But, the truth is that inhumane treatment, torture, isolation confinement, physical and psychological abuse, illegal detainment, murder, and so on routinely happened at the camps. Yet, the whole world turned a blind eye on these evil acts and the prisoners of the Viet Nam War. What happened to the Geneva Convention that the world hailed as its most sacred icon against bad treatment of prisoners? What about all the people who wanted South Viet Nam and the all good guys to play by the rules? Now they said nothing on behalf of the prisoners at these reeducation camps.

The world and its leaders seem to have a double standard when it comes to fighting evil and bad people. They make the good guys comply with their so-called sacred rules, but they let the bad guys get away with bad behavior too many times. Perhaps they are afraid to stand up against evil and simply let the innocent and the good guys fend for themselves. The South Vietnamese felt abandoned by the international community and betrayed by their allies, especially the United States of America. In their darkest hours, all their so-called friends and allies deserted them.

Even the critics and demonstrators against the Viet Nam War all disappeared after the war. They sided with North Viet Nam and became public propagandists for the Communists as they condemned any killing by the United States and South Viet Nam. And yet, they turned a blind eye to the horrible treatment and killing the Communists committed after the war. This hypocritical action and injustice the world and its leaders committed is one of life's lessons that Viet learned from the Viet Nam War. This could have made him bitter and angry and could have caused him to commit violent acts against the world, much like ISIS has done in recent years. However, he has chosen to live his life for a higher purpose and try to forgive and love others, even his enemies, as his Lord Jesus taught him.

It was ordered that papers and valuable information of the South Vietnamese government not to be destroyed, and it became a death sentence for all the service men and women of the South. The Communists used information against them without mercy. Worse yet, most ammunition and weapons were also kept intact. As such, most of the prisoners of the reeducation camps were deployed to move ammunition and weapons or disarm landmines and explosive ordinances. The Communists preferred that their enemies do that dirty work and potentially be killed rather than shooting them or gassing them and risking bad publicity and condemnation from the international community. That was how the Communists did not waste a bullet and continued to lie to the world about the camps. They led the world to believe they were wonderful in their treatment of prisoners and their citizens.

This is one of many lessons that Viet wished the world's diplomats, bureaucrats, and politicians could see and learn from the Communists. The Communist government consolidated power and took control over a sovereign republic in a short period of time without turning the takeover into a blood bath as we often see in other parts of the world. This is a life lesson that a politician or a general cannot learn at Harvard University or West Point Academy. Only by closely observing and living with the Communists could a person learn so much about their way of thinking, mode of operation, and ugly facts of life. Viet was lucky to learn this life lesson and became street smart to help him survive the Communists and the aftermath of the Viet Nam War. What he did not know is that there were still many more life lessons still waiting ahead of him.

An eye-opening lesson that Viet picked up during his initial experiences with the Communists was how they treated their enemies and the people they conquered. There had been rumors that the Communists were savage, cruel, and uncivilized. If they saw women with painted fingernails, for example, they would pull them all out. If they saw men with long hair, they would shave it all off. Viet apparently did not see anything like this happen, but what he saw happened around him made him sigh and told him a lot about the Communists' mode of operation. First, they confiscated all the properties of major institutions and big buildings, including Viet's private school, which was run by a group of nuns. They also announced that they would be taking measurements of each household and allowing people to only occupy so many square feet. The government confiscated the rest of the space. If a house was too big for a family, the Communists brought their own people to stay in that household without paying any rent. That was exactly what they did with many homes in Viet's neighborhood. His family scrambled around to bring in some relatives to live downstairs in their two-story home while they lived upstairs.

Another obnoxious thing the Communists did to the normal lifestyle of the Southern folks was that they would stop by any time of the day or night to take attendance of the entire household. They also conducted random security check to see if the family possessed any weapons or had any illegal possessions. Viet thought it was a joke when he heard of this random check. He thought there was no way that the authorities would barge into someone's home in the middle of the night—against the homeowner's will—and do anything they wished. But, it did happen to Viet's own family and many of their neighbors.

One late night when everyone in Viet's family was sound asleep, a series of loud bangs came against the door.

"Open the doors," heard Viet. "We need to take your household attendance."

"All right," Viet's mother responded. "We'll be right there."

She opened the doors and immediately everyone in her household, including his sisters and relatives, were awakened and rounded up for roll call. Viet saw several local Communist officials in his home that evening who carried out the raid. They searched the entire house, but thankfully they did not find any weapons or anything illegal. The whole search took about half an hour, but it seemed like forever as everyone stood silently in their pajamas. Viet's family also anxiously prayed that these officials would not plant any evidence to cause them trouble and arrest them. This ridiculous random search occurred several times a month in the middle of the night. Although Viet's family found this random search quite upsetting and unacceptable, they could do nothing about it. The only they could do was try to make it through the next day with help from above and find a reason to live in this nightmare.

Another crazy rule that the Communists created related to asking for permission to travel. If someone wanted to travel from one town to the next, one had to ask for permission. Otherwise, if the authorities came to your home to take attendance unexpectedly and did not find you, they would cross your name off the household roster, and you would lose your citizenship. Or, if the authorities caught you at your destination without proper permission for traveling, you would be thrown in jail and face all sorts of troubles.

This traveling rule applied equally to children and adults. Viet reflected on this rule and could not believe how ridiculous it was. One summer, he decided to go visit one of his uncles and aunts who lived in a village over a hundred miles away from Saigon. He could not believe that the authorities would make him get a permit for his trip. Thankfully, he received permission, because the authorities stopped by his home during his absence, and his mother showed them proper papers. Otherwise, he would have been in a lot of trouble. He also could have been stopped along the way and asked why he was traveling. The permit would clear him of any legal problems. He would not be suspected of trying to sneak out of the country illegally.

It was not just these ridiculous rules that Viet and his countrymen had to endure under the Communist regime. They also had to put up with Communist propaganda and patriotic music being broadcast throughout the neighborhood at least three times a day—morning, noon, and evening. Each session lasted at least an hour. They were forced to listen to all the "wonderful" things about Communism, its government, and patriotic songs. On the other hand, everything about the United States of America and the West was touted as evil and corrupt. Many country patriots fought their evil ways and shed their blood for that fight. This brainwashing propaganda went on nonstop every day. In today's world, this kind of propaganda would be labeled "fake news."

Sometimes, Viet thought he would need to check into a mental institution to find some peace and a cure from this Communist propaganda. Unfortunately, there were no such institutions. But, if there was one, everyone would fill the whole facility in a short time. In addition to the loud and annoying daily propaganda, everyone had to attend a mandatory neighborhood meeting once a week and hear more of the same propaganda. Viet often had to represent his family and most of that propaganda went right over his head. Any household that missed a meeting was fined, including jail time. Life with the Communists was like living out a death sentence. There was no future or hope. There were only misery and painful torture.

One of the worst things the Communists did to all Vietnamese was to turn neighbor against neighbor and one family member against another. Everyone had to watch what one said and did, especially if it was something negative about the Communists. Someone could turn you in, and you might end up in jail or get executed for something trivial such as making fun of the government. This seems similar to what has gone on in some countries in the Middle East. People did not know whom they could trust or who might stab them in the back and get them into trouble with the government.

Furthermore, there was no due process or a fair way for someone to appeal an injustice in this society. Because of the Communists, many family members turned against one another and sold out their beloved for a few pieces of silver. Viet remembered how his family in South Viet Nam constantly talked down their relatives in the north, where the Communists originated, and treated them like second-class citizens. They did not trust each other. Also, because of the Communists and the reeducation camps, some of Viet's friends also lost their fathers and had their families separated permanently. With their fathers imprisoned, some of Viet's friends' mothers married Communist officials and left their families turned upside down. It broke Viet's heart to see many of his friends' families face that pain and turmoil. Additionally, the children of a war have poor childhoods and a dim future to be what they want to be. This is one of the many hidden casualties of war that we humans, especially politicians, often do not recognize. This wound of war can indeed be much more painful and long-lasting than a physical wound.

Viet had just started his life with the Communists, but so far all he had seen was death, destruction, pain, suffering, threats, revenge, divisions, separation, turmoil, and hopelessness. He felt stifled and totally despondent. His life seemed to go nowhere and gradually headed towards a dead end. He thought he had awoken from a nightmare and had landed in a place that was completely desolate and lifeless, such as Hiroshima or Nagasaki. He found no signs of life either inside or outside of himself. He did not see any opportunities to better himself or any real dream that could come true in this land. He spent significant time reflecting and praying to determine reasons to live so that he could go on with his life. His loving Creator must have had reasons to bring him into this world and place him among the Communists. He tried to give his Creator the benefit of the doubt, and he tried to have an open mind about what the Communists might have in store for the youngest generation. He did not want to throw in the towel and give up on his life and future just yet.

It is always easy to quit and give in to life's challenges when things do not go our way. It is certainly less painful if we do not become tangled in the details of our daily life. But, what Viet would soon find out is that his loving God would never let him suffer or handle life's challenges alone. For God has always given him strength and has sent him the right people at precise moments to encourage him and lift him up. God wants Viet to live his life for a higher purpose and use God's gifts and blessings—not to keep all those blessings for himself, but to share them with others. By living his life this way, Viet would be able to survive any of life's challenges or deal with whatever problems life might send his way, even a horrible life with the Communists. What Viet did not know was that this wonderful life lesson would become a great foundation to make him a better and stronger person and help him survive.

Viet gradually began to search for reasons to live with the Communists and woke up every day seeing joy in simple and mundane things such as his first love, his simple faith, his small successes in school, and his daily good deeds. It is certainly difficult to find any joy and inspiration for someone whose life is under the control of the Communists. But, with prayer and reflection, Viet tried to find some joy and reason to wake up every day through something as simple as his first love.

Viet was in grade school and one of his favorite classmates was Lan Anh. They were assigned a seat next to each other in a classroom of more than 50 kids in a public school. Before this, he attended a private school, which was run by a group of nuns. When the Communists took over South Viet Nam, they shut down all private schools, confiscated many private and public institutions, and created public education from kindergarten to college. Viet had no choice and had to attend public school, but that was where he met his first love.

Lan Anh's home was on his way to school, and Viet stopped there frequently to do homework and play. Their families knew each other well and very much approved of this friendship. Viet certainly welcomed this friendship as a distraction from what was going on in his country, including the turmoil, hardship, suffering, uncertainty, and so on. This friendship brought him joy, comfort, stability, normalcy, companionship, love, hope, and much more. But most importantly, it brought him one more reason to live. He cherished this friendship and found himself very much at home in Lan Anh's home. Her family loved him and treated him as one of their own. They frequently invited him to stay for lunch or dinner. These two friends became like two peas in a pod, and Viet thought there was nothing that could separate them. Viet was convinced that he had found a great treasure in this friendship. This relationship was the source of comfort and encouragement for Viet during this period of distress and hopelessness.

Everything was going well with this friendship, and Viet could rely on it to bring him joy and hope and give him a reason to wake up every day. But, as mysterious as the friendship entered Viet's life, it unexpectedly disappeared. One early evening, Viet was at his dear friend Lan Anh's home to spend some time after school hanging around. Suddenly, her mother showed up and talked to Viet, saying, "Son would you come in the family room? I have something important to tell you."

Her voice and demeanor were quite serious. Viet did not know if he had done something wrong and was about to hear a long lecture about it. Or perhaps, one of Lan Anh's family members had contracted a serious illness, and her mother wanted to tell him to pray for him/her. He had also heard a little bit about pre-arranged marriages and mail-order brides as an Oriental custom. But he and Lan Anh were too young to get married. They were too young, even, to get a job. How could they support their family? He would have to quit school and find a job to take care of his young family. In fact, he had learned that his grandparents were married when they were fourteen or fifteen years old. If he said "no" to the marriage proposal, would her family ban him from seeing her ever again? Maybe the best way for him was to sneak out right now and avoid having to deal with this difficult and uncomfortable situation. He figured that eventually, her mother would forget about the whole thing and everything would go back to normal between him and her family.

Viet was filled with these and other anxious thoughts and did not know what Lan Anh's mother's urgent message might be. But, he obediently came into the family room and hoped for the best. Lan Anh's mother showed him a seat at a table in the middle of the room where her family usually gathered for dinner and said, "Son, please take a seat."

Viet quickly sat down and curiously asked, "What is going on, Mrs. Nguyen?"

She promptly responded. "Viet, you know that we've treated you like our own son. You and our daughter have been best friends for quite some time now." She was choked up, but overcame that overwhelming emotion and continued. "Unfortunately, Lan Anh and we are leaving for America soon. You see, her father left the county before the collapse of Saigon City with some American soldier friends and ended up living there ever since. Now, he is sponsoring our family to come to the United States of America to be with him. We're sorry to tell you about this news. But, we thought you should know, because you and Lan Anh have been best friends since kindergarten."

Viet was shocked by the news. He felt as if someone just put his or her hand into his chest and pulled out his beating heart. He did not know what to do or how to respond to this shocking news. He wanted to beg Mrs. Nguyen and say, *Please, don't go. Please don't take my best friend away from me!* But deep down, he knew he could not change her family's plan and stop his best friend from leaving for America—a country far away across the ocean. All he could muster at that moment were some broken thoughts.

With his voice shaking, he said, "Mrs. Nguyen, I totally understand. Thank you for letting me know about this." Then, he excused himself and exited the house. He went home and found himself in a quiet part of his home sobbing uncontrollably. It was as if he just heard the sad news of the death of a loved one. He did not know if he would ever see his best friend again. This was another casualty of the Viet Nam War that most people, including our politicians, would not know existed.

Just as someone who goes through different phases of grieving, Viet switched from feeling sad about the shocking news to getting angry at Lan Anh's father who showed up out of nowhere and caused a heart-breaking day for him. He wanted to curse and scream at his best friend's father. Then, he experienced an epiphany. During his time of friendship with Lan Anh, he had never seen her father. He assumed that maybe he was stuck in a reeducation camp like his own father and other men who worked for the South Viet Nam regime. The truth was that Lan Anh's father was one of the lucky people who escaped before the Communists took over Saigon and the entire South Viet Nam.

In some way, Viet was happy for his best friend and her family. They now had a way to get out of the hell hole and enjoy a better future. He was not quite sure where the United States of America exactly was. But, it must be quite a spectacular place, where the land is "flowing with milk and honey," like the Bible described the Promised Land for God's people. From this moment on, Viet began to search for anything that could tell him about the United States of America. He found an atlas and located it on the other side of the Pacific Ocean. But, it is miles away from Viet Nam. He also looked for reading materials in many American classic stories such as Jack and the Beanstalk, Little Red Riding Hood, Peter Pan and Captain Hook, and so on. The United States of America for Viet represented not only a romantic land for him to meet his best friend and first love again, but also the fairy tale, dream land where many magical, wonderful things remain to be discovered.

The next several days remained tense and difficult for Viet. He had to say goodbye to one of his best friends and first love and did not know if he would have ever seen her again. He had a tearful farewell with Lan Anh. With the lack of progress in communication technology at this time and the Communists' tight censorship, he sadly lost contact forever with this special person in his life. He walked by her home every day on his way to school and tried to reminisce all the sweet memories he shared with his best friend. Soon a new family bought that home. The sad loss of his best friend was compounded by the death of several dear people in Viet's life. His great-grandmother had been staying with Viet's family for several years. It is an Asian tradition that many generations of a family stay in the same household. That way, they can strengthen their family relationships and help each other a lot more. If an Asian family cannot take care of its older generation and ships that responsibility to a nursing home, they look shameful to their friends and neighbors. Caring for an elderly family member at home is not just a sacred responsibility but also a family honor. That is how a close-knit family shows love and respect to one another. That is how a nuclear family looks to the world in the Asian tradition.

Viet's great-grandmother just turned 100 years old a couple of weeks before his best friend Lan Anh's departure for America. He never met anyone who had lived that long before. But, having her in his home added flavor to his life. He spent more time with the older generation and learned how to take care of her. Viet remembered how she needed around-the-clock care. Viet had to help feed her, take her to the restroom, and bathe her. He felt sorry for her because she moved slowly, like a turtle, and was skin and bone. Amazingly, she was with Viet's family for more than a year. Unfortunately, not too long after Viet lost his best friend, his great-grandmother also died. He had just started to form a special bond with her due to the amount of time he spent with her and the constant care he gave her. Although it was a bit too much for a kid like Viet to look after his great-grandma, he felt that it gave him compassion for the elderly and taught him to take care of his family from an early age. Her death surely made him feel sad and created another hole in his aching heart.

But, that is how life on earth is. Sometimes, we must face one difficult thing after another and we wonder if we might be able to make it or not. Thankfully for us believers, we have our faith to give us comfort and guidance when we find ourselves in such situations. Viet relied on his faith to help him deal with difficult moments. He also counted on his faith to get him through the painful living under the Communist regime. His faith gave him strength and courage to face any difficulty in his life. Even though he had to face double losses—his best friend and his beloved great-grandmother—he did not let these losses overwhelm him or make him bitter. His faith helped him realize this was part of his imperfect life here on earth, and he learned to accept it graciously.

Unfortunately, the world could not see the amazing value of faith despite all the suffering and challenges happening daily. He recalled a wise person once said, "Don't pray that all your troubles will disappear. Pray that you'll have enough strength to deal with them." That was exactly how Viet would use his faith in dealing with daily difficulties and his depressing life with the Communists. His faith gave him endless power to survive one problem after another during those dark nights of his soul.

Viet so far had relied on his first love and his faith to help him survive the early days with the Communists and gave him reasons to wake up every day. But, those were not the only sources of strength that Viet could count on. He also tapped into little successes in school and daily good deeds for people around him to boost his spirits. These two things were like pain medicine that helped ease all the pain and trouble that he had to face daily.

Unfortunately, Viet face more troubles under the Communists' control. The first emerging troubles that Viet saw coming down on him and his countrymen was the contentious showdown between the Communists and neighboring countries such as China, Cambodia, and Laos. Around the Northern border, the Communists got tangled up with China, which was their ally at one time, but they were now on the brink of war with this neighbor. The Communist government began to amass thousands of troops along the border with China and recruited hundreds of young men and women for an impending war. The tension with this biggest neighbor created a huge economic burden and hardship on its citizens. China was one of the biggest trading partners with Viet Nam. Also, after the Viet Nam War, the country was isolated from the Western world and the economy and trading took a big hit as a result. But, picking a fight with China was just one of the emerging troubles that the Communists created for their citizens.

A bigger trouble that was looming during this time was the impending invasion of two other neighboring countries—Cambodia and Laos—by the Communist regime. One of those countries, Cambodia, was controlled by a notorious group call the Khmer Rouge. This government allegedly massacred millions of educated and innocent folks and was condemned by the entire international community. There were many mass graves in which thousands of bodies were buried. These evil places were called "The Killing Fields." The Communists apparently saw the Khmer Rouge as an impending threat to them and hence decided to invade Cambodia and Laos to drive out this notorious regime and establish their puppet government. By driving out the Khmer Rouge, the Communists did the world a big favor and put an end to the massive killing. They also recruited young men and women, many of whom were as young as fifteen, to carry out these wars.

Viet recalled that during the summer of his sophomore year of high school, he and many of his classmates were required to spend several weeks in basic training. They had to learn how to use all sorts of weapons such as bazooka, rocket propelled grenade (RPG), AK-47, M16, various grenades, baronet, and so on. Viet and his classmates also had to pick up techniques related to close combat and other basic training such as target shooting and the proper way to throw a grenade. Most of the students found these basic training weeks boring and unappealing. Some of Viet's friends even skipped this training and got themselves into trouble later with the authorities. Viet remembers that most of the girls in his class had a tough time holding up the AK-47 and other weapons with one hand as instructed on the training field and he felt sorry for them. Or, many of them were exhausted and passed out during the long runs and tough exercises of basic training. Still, all high school students were required to go through this basic training every summer.

However, required basic training was not the only thing the Communists imposed on their young and citizens. They also demanded that all high school students work for free at national exporting factories once a month during the school year. This free labor went on for the whole four years of high school. The students had to work with seafood and tropical fruits for eight hours straight with no break in factories with very bad working conditions. Viet remembers he once worked with pineapples, which was something he had rarely seen in the market. He curiously asked his supervisor why he could not find it available for daily use and was told that the country had to export this fruit to earn money, while the public had to consume other fruits. In fact, the people had to eat the core of the pineapple, which is usually discarded in other countries. But, it was not just withholding good fruit from its citizens, exploiting the young for free labor, or having a hawkish, war-desiring attitude toward its neighbors that the Communist government used to cause anxiety, fear, and worry among the citizens. It also gradually tightened its grip and control over daily life. They could not have public gatherings, discuss certain issues, do certain activities, possess certain consumer items, or travel beyond where they lived. Life with the Communists was like living out a death sentence and expecting the unexpected every day.

One beautiful, sunny day, Viet walked out on the back porch of his home and saw some of his family members and neighbors kneeling with their hands on the back of their heads. He knew his family was religious and prayed all the time. But, finding some of them kneeling in the middle of the backyard with their hands linked behind their heads was not the praying posture that he knew. As he stood watching these poor folks suffering under the hot sun and soaking in sweat, he wondered if he should go get some water for them. He approached a couple of them and asked, "Gentlemen, would you like some cool water to quench your thirst?" As soon as he finished asking, some Communist officials armed with weapons suddenly showed up in the backyard and told him to get away from the kneeling individuals and go back inside the house. Viet soon learned from his family that the Communists tried to conduct a random check in the neighborhood that day and simply wanted to intimidate citizens by subjecting folks to a humiliating punishment despite their innocence of any crime.

Viet could not believe the way the Communist government treated its citizens as he had just witnessed. They viewed them as possessions, sometimes like trash, and did to them anything they wanted. No one had any rights or a voice under the careful watch of the Communists. The public could not gather without the local authority's prior approval, and a friendly gathering should not be more than a handful of people. All religious services needed the same approval before any gathering could take place. And, the local authorities could shut them down at any time without giving proper reason. They also forbade anyone from listening to foreign music or radio broadcasting, such as the voice of America (VOA) or the British Broadcasting Corporation (BBC). Some of Viet's neighbors were caught listening to one of these forbidden things and were put in jail for a few days. The Communists were also the best at turning neighbor against neighbor and got everyone to report everything about anyone at any time. Viet could not see how he or any normal person could live under the control of the Communists. This was a tense and depressing time for Viet and many of his countrymen. He had to rely on his first love and friendship, his faith, his little acts of kindness, and his daily successes in school to give him reasons to live and wake up every day. These elements were part of Viet's higher purpose for living that helped him overcome all the challenges in his life. Without such a purpose, Viet would not have reason and strength to go on with his life under Communist control. But, he was not alone in adopting this life vision during tough times. All survivors of a tragedy or a horrible event share the same vision and thinking like Viet's to help pull them through that dark period of their lives.

Viet and many of his neighbors had searched for their higher purpose of living by going to a Christian church or a Buddhist temple every chance possible and finding comfort, guidance, and hope in quiet prayer time. Churches and temples were always packed with devout members every week. They also spent lots of time before and after services praying for their personal needs. Many went a step further and looked for miraculous saints to ask for their special intentions and find some peace and consolation in difficult or tumultuous times.

One of the popular saints was Saint Martin de Porres, who was black. Most Vietnamese had not seen dark-skin folks around them every day. But, apparently, he performed many miracles and helped many desperate folks get their prayers answered. He was born in Lima, Peru. His father was a Spanish knight and his mother was a black freed-woman from Panama. When Martin was only 12 years old, he became an apprentice to a barber–surgeon. At that time, barbers did not just give a haircut and a shave. They also treated the sick and dispensed medicines. After three years, Martin left that work to join the Dominicans—not to become a priest but to become a brother. He continued to dispense medicine to the sick and was put in charge of giving out the monastery's daily ration of food to the poor. He soon opened an orphanage and a hospital for foundlings (infants found after they were deserted by their parents). He also worked a great deal with African slaves who had been brought by ship to Peru; he visited them on the docks to comfort them and give them food and medicine. It was said that Martin helped anyone who needed blankets, shirts, candles, miracles, or prayers. He even helped animals by providing a home for stray cats and dogs at his sister's house. His shrine could be found at many churches besides the typical ones of Mary and St. Joseph.

During his life under the Communists control, Viet developed a good faith life and a close relationship with Jesus by watching how people around him coped with them and other challenging situations in their lives. Most of them relied on a higher power to give them strength and courage to go on. His faith gave him reasons to wake up every day and strength to overcome the difficult living conditions under the Communist government. It also became one of the secret weapons that helped Viet survive through life and gave him an edge over his opponents in a competition.

Besides his friendship and his faith, Viet counted on his personal successes in school, daily life, and sports to give him the boost that he needed in this challenging time. So far, life with the Communists only brought tears, sadness, despondence, suspicion, resentment, pain, and suffering. Everyone felt as if their lives had hit a dead end. Yet, Viet wanted his life to go somewhere and bring him some great promises. He worked hard in school and took special tutoring classes after school and in the summer to raise him to the top of his class and get all A's on his tests and class projects. He received one award after another throughout his school years. He was also one of the best athletes in physical education class and in many sports games, such as soccer, swimming, volleyball, badminton, and so on. In his time, he attempted to work on small jobs such as sewing clothes, tile work, construction, selling magazines, raising poultry, and so on to help his family make ends meet. He accepted piece work from local sewing stores and together with his mother, he helped sew parts of a shirt such as the collar, sleeves, the front or the back of the shirt, and so on. He also worked on braiding carry-on bags or assembling small tile pieces into a two-foot-by-two-foot sheet of different patterns. He tried to motivate himself to work hard and give himself a sense of success and accomplishment as he attended school full time and earned some income for his family. Perhaps, the Communists might want to control his dreams, but they would never succeed in destroying them.

Personal successes were not the only thing Viet tried to gather to bring him self-worth and a desire to live during this difficult period of his life. He also pushed himself to do good things for others, especially the misfortunate around him. There were plenty of opportunities for Viet to practice kindness and good deeds in the land of destruction and hopelessness. It seemed as if everywhere he turned, he found people in desperate need of help. He tried his best to reach out and do good deeds for everyone in need. He was certainly not required to be kind to others, and no one made him to do it. Viet soon learned that these acts of kindness not only made him feel good, but also gave him reason to live under the Communists and wake up every day. They helped show God's love and presence amidst a dark and broken world. He tried to help his family by going out to a neighboring well daily to get water for them. Noon was the best time to go to the well, because that was the hottest part of the day, and most people would try to avoid it. There would not be a big crowd of people at noon.

The well is typically a social gathering place for the whole neighborhood. Everyone comes there to get water and share stories of their lives. Children also come to the well to bathe and play on a hot day. That was how Jesus met the Samaritan woman at the well (John 4:5-42). He was thirsty under the burning heat of the sun and went to the well to get a drink. There he ran into the Samaritan woman who apparently also tried to get some water to quench her thirst. They started out in casual conversation and then switched to a spiritual and theological one. Jesus wanted her to think more about the spiritual water and eternal spring instead of the well water. Anyone who drinks well water will thirst again, but the spiritual water from the eternal spring will satisfy and quench one's thirst forever. Viet wanted this special water and found it in his faith and God's love. He always felt renewed and strengthened whenever he was in church and prayer or did a kind act for others.

At home, he also tried to learn how to cook for his family. He remembered the first time he cut his finger while cutting some vegetables. The wound was deep, and it hurt a lot. He was much more careful whenever he cut something after that. Or, once he opened the lid of a boiling pot and was not aware of the extreme heat of the steam. He was burned and learned to respect the steam much more while cooking. Or, when he first learned how to mix yeast with flour and bake his first loaf of bread for his family, he did not give the dough enough time to rise and the whole thing did not turn out good. Or, he had to learn to clean a fish or a batch of horseshoe crabs to make soup with tomatoes and bean sprouts, but the sharp gills or the pair of pincers cut and sliced his fingers to cause him bleeding badly after preparing this dish. However, he had learned to feel comfortable in the kitchen and can whip up any dish with his eyes closed. He could even tell when some restaurants undercooked their rice or put too much spices in their dishes whenever he went out for a meal.

By trying to cook for his family, Viet wanted to show them God's love and presence amidst their difficult life with the Communists. He made every effort to make someone's day a little brighter by going out of his way to be nice or sharing everything he had with others. This good habit gradually became second nature for him and stuck with him the rest of his life. Viet survived this difficult period of his life and made great strides in personal growth. He relied on his daily acts of kindness, his personal successes in school, his faith life, and his friendship or first love to deal with the dark and difficult days after the Viet Nam War.

His trust in the wisdom of his grandparents and ancestors also helped him learn to navigate his treacherous life with the Communists. Their wisdom taught Viet and his family to survive the last days of the collapse of Saigon city and continued to show them the way forward. Like many young people, Viet did not think much of the wisdom and knowledge that his grandparents and ancestors had acquired over the years. He did not know how useful all that stuff would be for him. But, slowly over time, he learned how wise his grandparents were and how much he longed to absorb all their past knowledge. He enjoyed sitting at their feet and gazing into their eyes to take in their amazing life stories and wonderful advice. He was reminded of someone else in the Gospel who did the same thing at the feet of Jesus. Mary, Martha's sister, was so fascinated by the wisdom and knowledge of Jesus that she simply sat at his feet to absorb everything and left all the mundane work, such as hospitality and house chores, to her sister. Like most people, Viet did not truly understand or appreciate what Mary did until he experienced the same thing in the presence of his grandparents.

Viet could not believe how much his grandparents had been through and learned from their past generations. They had to endure tough living with the French occupiers and later the Communists in North Viet Nam before migrating to the South. They learned French and lived under colonial rules for many years. Their lives and freedom were restricted in many ways. The Communists then defeated the French colonists and took over the north. But, their lives under the new regime did not get any better. Meanwhile, World War II broke out, and the Japanese took over most of Asia and ruled it with an iron fist as the Germans invaded the whole continent of Europe. The Japanese were so cruel and evil that millions of Vietnamese were starved to death. Many thousands more were killed during their occupation. Viet's grandparents shared stories of how the Japanese confiscated all the land that was used to grow rice and turned it into land to grow the materials to make bags and for the war. The result of that action was massive starvation and millions of people dead. The Japanese invaders also committed many other horrible atrocities, such as forcing local women to become their comfort companions against their will, enslaving thousands of local men to do the dirty work for them, or executing thousands of innocent people mercilessly to create fear and domination. Their cruel and merciless nature was so bad that Viet's grandparents preferred the French as their occupiers over the Japanese.

Thankfully, Viet's grandparents survived and escaped to South Viet Nam. Now, the Communists had caught up to them after defeating the United States and its allies in the South. His grandparents taught Viet many things about life survival and passed on to him this rule of thumb about dealing with the Communists: "Don't listen to what they [the Communists] say and promise. Rather, watch for what they do." Soon that would become the litmus test for Viet in dealing with politicians and all the relationships in his life. He became very suspicious of everyone and never trusted promises and flattering talk. In the days ahead, he came to prefer people who were real and could show concrete actions in dealing with him.

Chapter 3

Searching for God in the Land of Desolate

Faith has always been an important part of Viet's life. It was the reason he woke up every day after the war and continued to live under the Communists. It was also his source of strength and guidance in this time of confusion and uncertainty. What he did not know was that the Communists would not allow him and his countrymen to practice religion freely. He did not realize that the Communists were atheists. They did not believe in God or any organized religion. In fact, some Buddhist monks and believers had tried to collaborate with the Communists and thought that they would be treated differently compared to other religions and the rest of the citizens. Only later did they find out that the Communists still restricted their freedom of practicing Buddhism, and they put many prominent Buddhist monks and believers in prison without probable cause. Their arrest and others of well-known Catholic leaders brought outrage and condemnation from the international community. Clearly, life under the Communist regime increasingly got tougher with every passing day.

The church where Viet and his family attended had a deacon who seemed to do a lot of good things for the faith community and its individual members. He helped at church with Sunday services and taught religious classes for children and Bible study for adults. He also baptized babies, performed weddings, conducted grave-side services for funerals, visited homebound parishioners, and did several other activities for the faith community. All in all, he was a faithful deacon and a nice guy.

One day, Viet saw several Communist officials armed with guns surrounding the deacon's resident near the church and began to search his entire place. After a long search, which seemed to take forever, the authorities emerged with the deacon handcuffed and led him away without an explanation. Viet found out later that, for some reason, the Communists decided to get rid of the deacon, and they planted illegal weapons inside his residence to arrest him. We all knew that the deacon did not own or have any illegal intention to use those weapons. The beloved deacon of the faith community was set up and arrested. He would never be seen again.

Many religious leaders and regular citizens suffered the same fate at the hands of the Communists. In fact, Viet's pastor at the same church could not put up with the Communists and decided to sneak out of the country. The church did not have a pastor for a while. Many religious institutions such as seminaries and convents were also shut down and confiscated. The Communists did exactly what Jesus predicted His persecutors would do to Him and His Church. They attacked the leaders of the Church to rattle its members. Everyone basically was fearful about practicing their faith. They also tried to divide the faith community and get its members to turn against each other with false accusations.

No doubt it was difficult for Viet and his countrymen to go to church and live out their faith. He remembered one Christmas the faith community was not sure if there would be a service or not. This feast is one of the special Holy Days in Christian life, but the Communists threatened to close the church on this day. In case anyone does not know or forgets how the Communists work, everything that its subjects do, including breathing, must be approved and permitted before it can be carried out. Ironically, they never published any rules or regulations, and no one knew what they were. It always felt as if they made up rules as they went along. If they did not like something, they would stop it right on the spot. No doubt there was lots of corruption. If a person had money, he/she could bribe the authorities and get away with anything. Apparently, the Communists tried to give the members of Viet's church a hard time and decided to hold out on their permission to let them have a Christmas service. Everyone had to wait for more than two weeks for this decision. Finally, the day before Christmas Eve, the church learned that the authorities would allow them to do Christmas services that year. Everyone breathed a sigh of relief and began to get into the Christmas spirit by decorating the church with more lights and tinsel. However, they only allowed the church services to last only a couple of hours.

Christmas in a Communist country is not a public holiday as it is in the West. Children go to school and people work on Christmas just as they do on any typical day. In fact, Viet did not remember there were that many public holidays while growing up with the Communists. The only two holidays that everyone could be off work for a day and enjoy some time with one's family were the Lunar New Year (usually in February) and Independence Day (April 30). Although Christmas might not be a public holiday, this day was still very important to Christians living in a Communist country. It brought them peace and joy in a dark and depressing time of their lives. It was a special time for a group of believers to get together to celebrate the birth of their Lord Jesus and find some comfort in their faith, the Christmas carols, and their company. For Viet and his young friends, the midnight service was also a time for them to hang out late on a school night. Even though some of Viet's friends were Buddhists, they loved to attend this service annually and have a good time with their Christian friends. This spiritual service helped them and other Vietnamese forget the pain of living under the Communists' control and create some good memories out of their current horrible situation.

Karl Max, who was an atheist and a leader of the Communist and Socialist movements, often made fun of religion. He once said, "Religion is the opium or a special drug for the people." What he tried to say was that there is no God; people simply use religion as a means of escape and to avoid the harsh reality of life. That saying had come true for Viet and everyone who had to live and put up with the Communists. Without religion, people like Viet would take up drugs, alcohol, and other substances to numb themselves and ease their pain. But there is no pain pill on earth that can take away the amount of pain and suffering that Viet and his countrymen endured under the Communists.

Fortunately, tough times brought out the best in people and united people of different backgrounds into one loving family. Living with the Communists helped Viet and his Buddhist friends learn to work with one another and attend each other's services without any problem. The members of these two main religions shared mutual respect and care for one another. For they knew that there are a lot of good things that their religion could offer to the world, and their broken world could benefit a great deal from each—Christianity or Buddhism.

The rich and the powerful certainly do not need God's help and hence do not rely on God and religion that much. On the other hand, the poor and the lowly do not have anyone to protect and defend them. They need all the help they can get from anywhere, especially from high above. God is an anchor, a fortress, a compass, and a spring of water for these poor and lowly. While it was a challenge for Viet and his countrymen to search for God in the land of the Communists, their lives along a coastal area proved to be a test of faith during a certain time of the year. Like many coastal countries, Viet's homeland is usually a warm and paradise-like place with beautiful beaches. But, for several months at the end of the year, it could get bombarded by one tropical storm after another, often called typhoons. These storms can be quite destructive and deadly. When one of those hit the area, the wind gusts could get up to over 100 miles an hour, while heavy rain could go on for days and cause terrible floods.

Viet recalled walking to school in a flood that was as high as his waist. Sometimes, his whole school bag would be soaked in water and all his books and notebooks would be wet. Unfortunately, he wrote his notes in ink pen, instead of ballpoint pen, and everything was totally smeared. He could not tell his teacher that the dog ate his homework! Rather, he told his teacher the truth—that the rain smeared his homework. Those storms certainly added another level of misery and made it more challenging to find God in the land of the atheists. Like God's people who were exiled into slavery and the desert in the Old Testament, many South Vietnamese wondered where their Savior was and questioned if God still loved them. No doubt their faith was put to the test, and they were shaken to the core.

Thankfully, most people did not lose their faith. Rather, they went to church and temple regularly and got involved with their faith a whole lot. Viet and his family went to church twice every day in addition to their regular praying schedule—one at 5 am before school and another at 5 pm after school. They also participated in half an hour of devotional prayers before and after those daily church services. They spent much more time with church on weekends. Besides churches and temples, many people also flocked to miraculous sites to call for divine help and get their prayers answered. It seemed as if the more the Communists suppressed religion and tried to take it away from their citizens, the more people become involved with their faith and took it seriously. For that was the only thing left that the Communists still struggled to take it away from their subjects. They already took away their freedom, rights, possessions, future, and so on. But, they would not succeed in taking faith away from their people.

Like many people, Viet did not know how important faith was in one's life and appreciate all the miracles it brought to its believers. Only with time would he realize the value of faith and its magical power in the life of its believers. To his surprise, he witnessed one of the amazing miracles that faith did for his family. Like many families that lived with the Communists, Viet's family struggled to keep food on the table for its members. Even though they had money, the country was short on food and supplies; hence, they could not buy much of anything. Furthermore, the Communists allowed each family to store up only a certain amount of food. Some food items, such as sugar, were considered a national treasure, and each family could only keep a small amount in the home. If the authorities caught someone storing up more food than the allowed amount, everything would be confiscated and the person would be put in jail.

Viet's family managed to feed the entire household since the end of the war from their rice container without any problem. He came to get rice from the container every day to prepare meals for them and was never worried that the container would get empty. One day, Viet opened his family rice container and was surprised to find just enough rice for one more meal for his household. He felt a big knot in his stomach and wondered where his family would get rice for their next meal.

This accident reminded him of the story of the widow in Zarephath in the Old Testament (1 Kings 17:10-16). Apparently, the whole region was hit by a severe drought and the harvest was poor. The food supply was scarce. A widow and her only son were preparing their last meal together when a stranger named Prophet Elijah showed up at the door of their house asking for something to eat and drink. Instead of refusing to share their little amount of food with this stranger and turn him away, they invited him to stay and eat whatever food they had without worrying about tomorrow. Their generosity and trust in God reached the Heaven and God used the Prophet Elijah to perform a miracle for them. Their jar of flour never ran low, but lasted them for a whole year. But, it was not the only miracle that Viet heard about in the Bible or the last miracle that God would have ever done in our world. To his surprise, Viet would soon experience the same miracle in his own life.

Since the end of the Viet Nam War, Viet's faith in God took root and developed. As his life under the Communist government became difficult and uncertain, he had to search for support and protection wherever he could get it. He could not trust the Communists to defend him or give him help. They seemed to create more chaos and havoc for their citizens than helping them. There was also no hero figure like Robinhood or a knight on a white horse around to restore peace and justice for the folks who were under the yoke of the Communists. Naturally, Viet came to God and relied on his faith to give him guidance, bring him comfort, provide him daily support, and lift his spirit with some spectacular miracles. He had already experienced an amazing miracle by his surviving of the violent end of the war. He would be blessed with another miracle as the Lord helped keep his family's rice container from getting empty.

Everyone knows that the main diet for most Asians is rice. Unfortunately, under the Communist government, supplies were scarce and families were not allowed to store up much of anything. Viet's family could not stock up enough rice and found their rice container one day ran low. They barely had enough rice to one last meal. They would run out of food and face starvation and imminent death, much like the story of the widow of Zarephath and her only son.

Viet did not know what he had to do or where he could find rice for his family in the coming days. He also did not want to alarm them and make them worry about this desperate situation. He began to pray and asked God to give his family a helping hand and perform a miracle for them. Viet had never used prayer to ask God to intervene and perform a miracle before. He often prayed for something, but not a life-saving miracle like this for his family. After a couple of days asking God for help, his prayer seemed to be answered. Suddenly, the local authorities decided to move up the distribution date for the public and let the community purchase their monthly supplies earlier. They also increased the amount of rice that each family could get. Viet's family got their necessities and filled up their empty rice container just in a nick of time. He never told his family about this amazing experience. But, truthfully, that day he was blessed to experience one of many miracles in his life. It opened his eyes to see that there is a loving God who does listen to God's people's prayers, especially the cry of the poor.

This miracle healed Viet's blindness and helped him see many other miracles in his life. It let him know that God is always present in our world, even in the toughest, darkest moments of our lives. Unfortunately, some might have allowed the world and other bad influences convince them otherwise and drive them away from their loving God. But, that is a terrible mistake if we want to survive this life and make it to the next. God is our best source of help and protection on earth. Viet gradually realized that hidden treasure and its amazing power in his life with the Communists. Life under this government was extremely difficult and only God could help him through this dark night of his soul. God also could guide him through all sorts of other tough situations in the future. By having a good, strong relationship with God, Viet had the courage and confidence to deal with future challenges. He also had the humility and compassion to help people in need around him. After all, they reflect the image of his loving God, and he must show his love for God not by talking about it, but by treating them with care and compassion.

Chapter 4

Searching for Humanity in the Pile of the Outcast

Viet learned from the Bible that God made human beings in God's image, and Viet deeply believed in it. He tried to hold up that belief throughout his life and treat his countrymen with respect and compassion no matter how difficult that could be at times. That belief would be put to the test as the whole country had to face scarce supplies, a poor economy, and the aftermath of a destructive war. Everywhere Viet looked, he saw the scars and damages of the Viet Nam War. He saw beggars and panhandlers at every street corner, while drug addicts passed out on the roads drooled over a pile of needles and meth paraphernalia. There were also many folks who lost arms and legs due to the war trolling around all over Saigon city and throughout his neighborhood. Adding to this mosaic tapestry of war consequences, Viet witnessed daily the hideous look of lepers, long lines at grocery stores, big crowds at movie theaters, a lack of medicine at nurse stations, and so on.

Everyone knows that war is destructive and costly. The price of the Viet Nam War was beyond any dollar amount and could be seen all over the country. Most buildings were pocked with bullet holes, while playgrounds were scattered with in-explosive ordinances, military equipment, and piles of rubble. Everyone seemed to carry a scar of this war in one way or another. Some had to walk around with a lost limb, while others had a weary look that made them age beyond their years. Everyone was hurt in some way and quite weary about their future. They did not know what their future would be like or where their next meal might come from.

One of the first consequences of the war was the lack of necessities and daily supplies. During the war, people destroyed things and stopped growing or building things that would improve their lives. They wasted valuable time fighting, and it would take years for them to catch up with the rest of the world and rebuild what was destroyed. Daily necessities were scarce and people had to ration every little thing. Besides that, the Communist authorities tried to manage the flow of daily supplies to control the life of its people and make them do what they wanted. This allowed only certain things to be sold to the people and announced an assigned date for people to buy them. If someone forgot about that date and showed up late for the item, the line for it would be so long that it would sold out by the time his or her number was called. Everything under the Communist system typically involved long lines and endless waiting.

Sometimes, a person had to spend the whole day waiting to get some rice. The next day, one would do the same for some sugar or salt and eventually used the entire month to get some basic supplies for his or her household. This was in addition to getting materials to fix clothes or doing house maintenance. Even a trip to a local movie theater proved to be quite an ordeal as one would have to wait for hours to get a ticket. The waiting line for a movie ticket or some basic supply could wind through several neighborhood blocks. Fights and arguments under the tropical heat were a common thing. Viet had to turn around and go home after not being able to acquire a ticket for a popular movie. To help him cope with long waiting lines and the frustration it caused, Viet trained himself to pick up the virtue of patience and tried to practice it daily. This virtue helped him learn to take one day at a time and do everything he could with the help of God. It also kept him calm and got him not to get mad in dealing with the bureaucracy of the Communist government. Patience was the divine medicine that he needed at this point in his life.

Lacking supplies meant that people stole, cheated, robbed, and tricked their neighbors to get what they needed. It was simply about survival. However, Viet learned from his Christian faith and the Bible that all those things were wrong even though it was all about survival. It does not matter how desperate one's life might be; one cannot cheat or take something from one's neighbor without his or her permission according to Christian teachings. Unfortunately, Viet witnessed all those sinful things happen around him every day. He saw people pickpocket others in crowded places. He was told how someone could rob a watch from a traveler by using certain techniques. It was a common occurrence for Viet to see desperate people cheat and trick one another in an outdoor market or on a street to get something and stay alive. In fact, Viet had a personal experience about this as he was waiting at a bus station for a relative coming to visit his family one day.

It was a warm, beautiful morning and Viet went to a bus station to pick up a relative with his uncle. They were having a pleasant conversation and talking about the joy they would have upon seeing this long, lost relative. They had not seen this relative for years, and they did not know if they would be able to recognize him or not. As the arrival time for the bus was approaching, Viet's uncle told him to watch over their bicycle while he went inside the bus station to see if the bus would arrive on time or not. He left for just five minutes and suddenly a stranger approached Viet and told him that his uncle was calling for him inside of the bus station. Viet believed in the genuine goodness at the core of each human being and the importance of being obedient to God's commandments. He did not think the desperate times of living with the Communists would drive people to trick and steal from their neighbors. So, he left the bike with the stranger and went to look for his uncle. But, as soon as he saw his uncle, he was told that he was not called for. Viet quickly realized that he was duped and that the stranger just stole their bicycle. They ran outside to catch the thief, but it was too late. The thief had already disappeared with their beautiful, expensive bicycle.

Viet felt horrible for letting down his uncle and quite sad about losing that bicycle. He was also angry at the thief for violating God's commandments and cheating his neighbor. That day, Viet's total trust in humanity took a big hit, and it would take him a long time to restore his trust in another human being. He could not believe his homeland would be that desperate to turn someone against his or her neighbor. He did not know if he should take on a different attitude toward humanity from that moment forward and become mean, angry, rude, indifferent, careless, or unmerciful in dealing with another human being or not. One thing for sure is that his faith in humanity took a big hit after that bike was stolen. The Communist government already tried to turn one neighbor against another and now one of Viet's countrymen betrayed his trust and hurt him like that without regret. He felt disheartened by this terrible experience and wondered how low people would go to hurt one another after living with the Communists for a while.

Perhaps that stealing incident put his trust in humanity to the test. Luckily, Viet's compassionate heart for humanity was not swayed that easy. His caring attitude was overwhelmed by what he saw around him every day. The first sad and heartbroken sight for Viet was a group of painful-and-hideous-looking people who often passed by his neighborhood begging for food. Some of them were adults and others were kids. Their faces and hands were filled with ooze and red blotches. Some of them bled badly and looked quite painful. They had contracted leprosy. Viet truly felt sorry for these folks and tried to give them money or anything he might have to ease some of their pain. He recalled once he was holding an orange and wanted to eat it badly. Suddenly, one of these poor lepers showed up asking for some food. It was a little kid whose face was covered with bleeding sores and terrible ooze.

Viet checked everywhere to find some money or food to give him. The only thing he found was the orange in his hand. Viet's eyes welled up with tears, because he was embarrassed about not being able to help this kid, and he felt sorry for him. In America, a panhandler might beg for some help, but he or she really wants money, not food. In other poor countries like Viet Nam, a panhandler does not choose money over food. He or she will take any help to keep him- or herself alive. Like Jesus in the Gospels, Viet's heart was moved with pity for this child beggar. He wondered what the kid did to deserve that horrible fate. He was also curious about how the kid's future would turn out. He put the orange in the kid's dented tin bowl and gentle said: "Sorry, that's all I have." The leper's mother joined him at that moment, and they both said: "Thank you. That's ok!"

Viet later found out that those hideous-looking beggars were lepers. These folks were mentioned a lot in the Gospels. They were outcast and rejected by society even back then. Everyone thought that leprosy was contagious; hence, society did everything to shun them. No one wanted to be near a leper except Jesus. He reached out to them, touched them, and healed them. He showed them that He loved them and cared for them unconditionally. Most important, He let them know that they were made in the image of God, and they should be treated like any other human being. Unfortunately, we humans cannot change our attitude that easily. Even in modern times, everyone still treats lepers like aliens and keeps them far away. Viet

Nam is one of the countries that has reserved one of its islands exclusively for lepers. It is not because it thinks highly of lepers and wants to give them special treatment. Rather, it simply wants to push these poor folks far away from civilization and hide them on some island—God's forsaken place. Life on the island apparently was a bit too exclusive and not that glamorous. Some decided to risk the dangerous trip across the ocean and return to the mainland to find a new life. Unfortunately, most of them often did not have much with which to start that life, and the Communist government did not help them at all. They usually ended up as street beggars.

Along with these street beggars and lepers, Viet also saw drug addicts who would often pass out on a pile of needles and other substances. One of their sleeves would be rolled up and tied with some sort of string through which they would insert a needle. There were also lots of drunk people wandering the streets of Saigon city every day. The sight of beggars, lepers, drug addicts, and drunks on the streets was almost like a zombie movie after a catastrophic event or Dooms day. That sad and hopeless scene was what Viet saw every day. He witnessed it on the way to school, church, market, park, and so on. It looked so depressing and heartbreaking that he tried to look away or pretended it was not there.

We humans tend to push anything we do not like under the carpet and avoid dealing with it. But, this ugly scene showed up day after day. He could not avoid it anymore and had to figure out how to deal with it. It is certainly a sad and difficult reality of life with the Communists. He could choose to be heartless, uncaring, and indifferent to the plight of the poor and the misfortunate around him. Or, he could try to be caring, concerned, and compassionate with them. After much prayer and internal struggle, Viet chose to be a person of love, care, and compassion to others and try to be like Jesus to the broken world around him. Perhaps it might take him years to master these virtues, but he wanted to start working on them now and making them an essential part of his daily life. By doing that, he would be on the right path in his search for meaning and purpose of his life on earth.

During this time of his life, Viet was also put in a tough situation as he was asked to take care for one of his aunts, who evidently was suffering the last phase of breast cancer. After the collapse of

Saigon city, the Communists took over the whole country and began to close churches and temples, confiscate their land and buildings, and arrest and displace thousands of priests, deacons, nuns, monks, and seminarians. Many of them left their religious institutions and went home to their families or lived in hiding.

This aunt of Viet's had to leave her convent and went home to hide herself from the Communists after they closed her convent. She avoided the authorities and its persecution of religious leaders for several years by hiding at home. Now she was succumbing to a deadly disease. In modern times, people can beat this cancer and live free of it for years if it is identified early and treated in time. Unfortunately, Viet's aunt did not undergo an annual mammogram to catch this cancer early. She did not feel well one day, and the family called a doctor for a secret home visit in the middle of the night. The entire visit was almost like a scene out of a Wild West movie, when a doctor is summoned in secret to see an infamous gun fighter who is hurt and hiding in some hotel room in town. This trusted doctor paid Viet's aunt a home visit, but unfortunately, he gave the family very grim news of her condition. They were told that her cancer was in the last stages, and there was no cure for her. It was just a matter of time before she would take a last breath. But no one knew when that moment would come.

Once again, Viet was called to take care of his sick aunt. He previously helped look after his great-grandmother, but he never dealt with a cancer patient or knew how to comfort a dying person. Living in a war-torn country, Viet was not a complete stranger to death. However, this time death seemed to be personal and weighed heavily on his heart. He wanted to cry every time he was near her because of her helpless condition. He could see the pain on her face and wished that he could take it away from her. Her pain seemed to reflect the pain that the rest of the country had to endure under the Communists. Every time Viet lifted her up for a drink or something to eat, her entire skinny body would ache with excruciating pain. Or, when he had to help her get to the bathroom, that short trip would almost turn into the long journey of Jesus to Mount Calvary. It was painful, slow, and extremely long for her. Viet recalled several weeks before she was quick and nimble and had no problem getting to the bathroom by herself. Now she needed another person to help her and still had a tough time getting there. It broke Viet's heart to see his favorite aunt looking like that.

Viet will never forget the time he tried to lay her down on the bed after coming back from the bathroom. Instead of gently putting her down, he dropped her like a hot potato on the traditional wooden-frame bed that most Vietnamese sleep. He did not intentionally drop her out of frustration or anger. Rather, he was a little kid and could not hold on to anything for a long time. Before he could apologize, his aunt cried out in paid and said, "Are you trying to kill me or what?" Viet jokingly responded, "I'm so sorry. You caught me red-handed doing that. You see, I couldn't fool you." Then, both busted out laughing.

At first, Viet could not see the value of helping his suffering aunt other than the fact that it was his duty to do so. But, as days turned into weeks and he began to settle in with his daily care duties, Viet gradually realized that what he was doing would help shape his character and make him a caring and compassionate human being. Most people do not like to take care of a sick person and help someone in need. Worse yet, some might even be indifferent and heartless toward the plight of other suffering human beings, who were made in God's image and are their brothers and sisters as far as Jesus their Lord is concerned. Because of such an attitude, our world has turned a blind eye to many horrific and outrageous tragedies such as the Holocaust, the massacre by the Khmer Rouge, the starvation of millions of people due to wars and famine, neglect for the proper care and education of the young in inner cities, and so on. By taking care of his sick and dying aunt, Viet gradually realized the truth about real life and developed compassion for the suffering and the afflicted. Real life is full of pain, suffering, tears, and sadness. A caring and compassionate person understands that and tries not to cause any more hurt and headache to everyone around. Rather, one would learn to lessen the pain of others and reach out to bring comfort and healing to his or her broken world.

The world that Viet saw after the war was not only broken and hurting but also quite cunning and deceptive. It was a dog-eat-dog world, and many people did not hesitate to cheat, lie, trick, and hurt his or her neighbors to get what he or she wanted to survive. Everyone jostled, pushed, tripped, and climbed over one another to get a loaf of bread, a piece of meat, a bag of rice, some fresh fruits and vegetables, a bar of soap, or a liter of kerosene.

That was exactly what Viet saw playing out day after day on the streets of Saigon City. Everyone tried to survive by tricking or outplaying his or her neighbors. One of the ways to do that was to make fake or poor-quality products. Viet had to learn to figure out if a product was fake or bad by tapping and carefully examining it. Most imported products from the United States, France, Germany, Italy, Spain, or Japan were always good and reliable. Unfortunately, some local business people took counterfeit products and put foreign tags on them.

Viet could tell the genuine products from the fake ones by listening to the pings from his taps. For example, a genuine foreign-made body of a bicycle would hold together and mostly be intact after a collision compared to a locally made one. He would tap several times on the metal frame and pause to listen to the pings. The genuine one would have a solid sound, while the fake one would have a hollow sound. He had to learn all these tricks and apply these skills to get good and long-lasting products for his family. He applied a similar testing process for all items, including the foods and fruits he bought for his household.

Going to shop in a grocery store in America is easy compared to grocery shopping in Asia. Everything in the Western world is already priced and quality approved. On the contrary, most of the items bought in Asia must be bargained in an outdoor market. Everyone goes shopping daily to get fresh food because of the lack of refrigeration systems and storage. Price bargaining is an art. A good bargainer will not offer the opening price too high because he or she might end up with a steep price for a product. On the other hand, a shopper should not open with an offering price too low, because the seller might consider it an insult and get mad to the point of cursing you. But, that is just a small part of the whole complicated shopping ritual that a family in Asia must go through every day.

Another difficult part is knowing how to tell good products from bad ones. Viet Nam does not have the Food and Drugs Administration (FDA) to set standards and test products before anyone can sell to customers like we do in America. As such, most products are not guaranteed and are purchased at one's own risk. Viet had to figure out if a watermelon was sweet and not bad inside by reading its stripes and observing its look on the outside. He learned how to do that with all the fruits and vegetables. Certainly, it took a long time for Viet to get good products to prepare a nice meal for his family every day. By learning how to bargain well and figure out good products from the bad ones, Viet acquired a great set of skills that would serve him well in the future.

The whole process of learning those important skills made Viet realize that the world around him was quite cunning and selfish. Everyone simply focused on one's own needs and did not think twice about the plight of one's neighbors. In fact, people would not have any problem taking advantage of their neighbors and stepping over them to get what they wanted, even to the point of hurting them. Viet gradually learned to be street smart and began to become like the world by stepping over others to get what he wanted. He got everything a teenager would ever dream of, including motorcycles, Rolex watches, nice clothes, televisions, and other electronic toys. He was at the top of his game and enjoyed every moment of it. Like the rest of the world, Viet did not feel the pains of the people that he trampled on or care if he had to trick them to get what he wanted. For him, it was simply a game of survival. He made up excuses to numb himself from feeling the painful losses of others. He felt that if he did not get material possessions by tricking people, the Communists or someone else would get them.

Viet had an internal battle between the survival skills he learned from the world and the compassionate attitude he picked up through his Christian upbringing and caring for his sick family members and other misfortunate folks on the streets. Fortunately, God came to Viet's aid and helped him figure out which way of life he should turn away from and which one he should embrace. This was one of many moments of conversion that Viet experienced and saw God's grace working in his sinful life. Like St. Paul and St. Mary Magdalene, who turned away from their sinful ways of life with the help of God's grace, Viet turned away from his former lifestyle of tricking and taking advantage of others for his own selfish gain and coming home to the Lord. His moment of conversion happened during an encounter with another young man in his neighborhood.

There was a young man who sold ice cream in Viet's neighborhood. He was one of the favorite people among all the neighborhood kids. They all came out to greet him and buy their favorite ice cream from him. They knew when he would come, and they would be ready to gather around him. Viet and his siblings were no exception, and they would come to the ice cream man for that delicious treat on a warm, muggy day. All the neighborhood kids usually had money to pay for their ice cream. But, they were not always good at setting aside their money for that special treat, and sometimes would not have any money left for it. But, this ice cream man trusted Viet, his siblings, and the other neighborhood kids to let them buy ice cream with an "I owe you" (IOU) and pay him later. Sometimes, he even let the whole neighborhood have whatever he could not sell without charging them anything.

Viet watched the ice cream man and was surprised by his trust and generosity. He could not believe that there were still kind and generous people like him in a dog-eat-dog world like Communist Viet Nam. So far, all Viet had learned from the world was to be cunning, deceptive, heartless, uncaring, and indifferent to other people. The world even encouraged Viet to take from his neighbors whatever he wanted. After being tricked by a stranger at a bus station and losing his uncle's bike, Viet also slowly lost any trust in humanity. He was certainly going down the wrong path and did not know if he should trust and care about another human being. He thought that the only one he should care about was himself and no one else. Fortunately, God used the ice-cream man to restore Viet's trust in humanity and develop in Viet a sense of care and compassion for others. The ice cream man was the Guardian Angel that God sent to Viet to open his eyes and bring him back to the right path.

We might not realize this, but God often sends many kind folks to us as God's angels to help us throughout our lives and show us the way to God. We might assume that God is hands-off from our world and everything that happens in it. The truth is far from that. God continues to offer help and reach out to us through everything that goes on in our daily lives. Perhaps, we might not realize this. But, if we take a step back and rely on the eyes of faith and prayers to help us look at the big picture, we will surely see God's footsteps in our lives. There are all kinds of signs of God's presence around us. Angels are the most obvious sign of them all. Unfortunately, we usually picture angels as a special creature with wings and a halo. But, the truth is that angels look just like you and me and are sent to us with a special mission from God. They are sent to give us a hand and show us God's love and presence in our world. Hopefully, by our encounter with them, we focus our lives on something higher than mundane things like money, fame, glamor, material things, accomplishments, or appearance. That higher goal or purpose will give meaning to our lives and help us get out of bed and move forward every day. It also gives us courage and strength to deal with the dark nights of our souls or tough challenges in our lives.

So far in his life, Viet relied on the wisdom and guidance of his grandparents and ancestors and the kind support of the angels God sent him daily to help him deal with the Communists and continue to survive each day with hope after the Viet Nam War. His grandparents and ancestors passed on the experiences, life lessons, traditions, and wisdom to him and the future generations of his family. These folks had been through life, made mistakes, and survived awful experiences to share many valuable lessons with the next generation. They are like good counselors who will tell us what might be a good thing or bad one for our lives. They are like kind coaches who can warn us what we need to avoid and what we need to do more. They are like caring teachers who advise us which tradition we should keep and which one we must let go. They are like our best friends who love us uncondi-tionally and will always be by our side in the most difficult moments of our lives to comfort us and lift us up. Viet's grandparents and ances-tors had taught and advised Viet not to settle and focus on earthly things like material possessions, money, fame, glory, vanity, and accomplishments. For those things would not last in tough times and would let him down in the long run. Rather, he should aim for higher purposes as his life mission and be the reason to wake up every day. If Viet could do that, he would not become disillusioned, hopeless, depressed, heartbroken, or disappointed when his life changed or took a wrong turn. For Viet, that higher purpose is Jesus and helping oth-ers, especially the poor and the misfortunate. So far in his life, that purpose had given him hope and reason to go on with his life under the tight control of the Communists.

Another important lesson that Viet learned during his difficult days with the Communists is that God sends good people throughout our lives to help, guide, comfort, and point us to the right direction. These people are like angels that God sends us to bring us God's love and give us a hand. They tell us what we need to do and reassure us that God is still with us in the darkest moments of our lives. In Viet's case, God sent him an angel in the form of a kind and generous ice cream man to restore his faith in humanity and help him learn to be a kind, caring, generous, and compassionate person. Without that angel, Viet might still be on the wrong path into which this cunning and mean world had tried to lure him and turn him into a cold, deceptive, selfish, and uncaring person. That was the first angel that God has sent Viet's way. Thankfully, he recognized the angel without lots of prayer and reflection. Viet certainly cherished and appreciated the presence of angels in his life.

Chapter 5

Searching for Identity and Life Mission in the Wasteland

South Viet Nam after the collapse of Saigon City was the land of tears, sadness, destruction, fear, and hopelessness. Life was hard from day to day. No one knew what tomorrow might be like or if one might live until tomorrow. Everything was uncertain and heading nowhere. Every day, Viet woke up and felt like a big, dark cloud was following him, even though his country was usually a paradise-like, tourist destination with blue skies and beautiful beaches. He did not know who he was and what he was supposed to do with his life. He tried to fill his day with endless activities to keep himself busy and numb himself from all the pain of living with the Communist government. He went to school for most of the day for six days a week. After school, he did some extracurricular activities such as taking private tutoring courses to stay ahead in his classes and going to church. Finally, he tried to help at home with chores such as getting water at the well, cooking, washing clothes and dishes, and so on. That was what most of his days were like week after week. This vicious cycle continued throughout his middle and high school years. It felt as if his life was stuck, and time seemed to stand still. Nothing he did seemed to make a difference in his life or the lives of other people around him.

Unfortunately, during this time of turmoil and uncertainty, Viet was basically running his house as "the man of the house" while his mother was working outside of the house to earn a living for the whole family. His father was held in a reeducation camp, which was created for members of the former regime and run by the Communists. Viet saw his father once a year. His camp was also changed often without any notice; therefore, often they did not know where he was. It was up to Viet's family to pay the authorities and do their own investigations to find out where his father was detained. The reason they moved his father around was because they did not want these prisoners to figure out how to escape and to make his family bribe them to find out where he might be kept. His father looked thin, dark, sad, and depressed every time Viet visited him at the camp. Viet learned that his father had to plant a garden and outsmart his interrogators in the camp to survive day to day. His father also tried to determine his life's mission to make it through his difficult moments in those detention places and keep his hope for living alive. Like his father, Viet did some soul searching to figure out what he was supposed to do with his life in this new world order. This was the beginning of a life-long process for him to discover his own potential and what he would be called to do for the rest of his life.

The first thing for Viet to do in the process of discovering his potential and figuring out his life's mission was to test his intellectual ability and see how well he could do with his mind. Since kindergarten, Viet always took his school work seriously and enjoyed learning. He loved to take in new knowledge and compete in school. Most kids do not like school and think it is a bunch of nonsense and useless information. But for Viet, school was always fun, and he wanted to learn how the world worked, how God fits into Creation and humanity, and what he could do to contribute to society. He loved to grab any books he could get his hands on and start reading. Under Communist control, Viet Nam suppressed freedom of information and turned into its neighboring countries like China of the 1960s and Cambodia of the 1980s. With the Cultural Revolution in China, its Communist leader Mao tried to wipe out intellectual knowledge by burning most of its books. The Khmer Rouge did the same thing in Cambodia and went a step further by killing its teachers and educators. Viet Nam might not go to the extent of its two neighbors to control intellectual knowledge and information, but its authorities censored and limited its people to reading only certain books and reading materials. There was no public library or bookstore available for people to get access to knowledge and world news. If the authorities caught its people possessing any banned materials, they would be put in jail and the materials would be confiscated. The banned materials could be anything that put the Communist government in a bad light or something that might make Americans and Westerners look good. Viet and most of the school kids were constantly bombarded and brainwashed about the atrocities committed by the American troops during the Viet Nam War. They were regularly required to visit the mocked-up atrocity sites the

Communists created to propagandize their anti-American/Western agenda. These sites were filled with horrible and disturbing images and artifacts.

Beside controlling reading materials and manipulating how information flowed into and out of their country, the Communist government also dictated the focus of its educational system. The core subjects that all high school students were required to study for at least four years were mathematics, physics, chemistry, biology, basic composition, and a foreign language. The government believed that these subjects were a good foundation of knowledge and provided opportunities for future learning for the young. In the beginning, most students hated that core curriculum schooling. It was difficult and quite demanding. Each subject of the core curriculum was typically at the college level and many students had to pay to attend tutoring courses outside of class in the evening and during the summer to understand the material a little more and get better grades. Most high school students did not have time for anything else except studying. The foreign language requirement of the core curriculum education system divided many friendships, because students were assigned randomly to one of the three main languages, namely, English, French, and Russian, when they attended high school. Most of Viet's friends were divided into different classes, because they had to take up a different language. There was also gym and sports time under this school system, but it was emphasized less compared to the American school system. That is why the Olympic Games and sports were considered trivial in the eyes of the Communists. Additionally, the school week extended for six days—Monday to Saturday—and the school year lasted for more than nine months without any breaks at all. The intensity of this educational model scared many students and caused them to hate school. But, indeed, they did not have any other choice.

Although the core curriculum was quite difficult and demanding, Viet rallied to this challenge. He gradually appreciated how rounded it helped shape his learning and future knowledge. This exact system has been used in some world-class school systems such as the Japanese and German. Unfortunately, in America, the core curriculum has been quite controversial and criticized. People assume it would take away parents' input and be controlled by liberal thinking. This might be true in dealing with English Composition or Writing and the materials selected to be used for that class. Or, perhaps, sex education might be used to promote a certain political viewpoint and give our children mixed messages. Otherwise, Viet could not understand how some important subjects such as mathematics, chemistry, physics, biology, and languages might get manipulated for a political agenda. They simply pass on the facts and knowledge of past experiences. They do not have any political viewpoint.

Viet believed that the core curriculum gave him a broad range of knowledge and made him a well-rounded person so that he could explore many interests and career options in the future. It is ironic for critics of the core curriculum to throw the whole thing out without doing diligent research and talking with someone like Viet who experienced it first-hand to evaluate the whole program on facts and not on unfounded fear. They could keep most of the important subjects above and change how English Composition or Writing picked its reading materials.

Despite some positive things about the Communist educational systems such as the core curriculum and its spending cost per student, it had some flaws like any manmade thing. It spent less than a couple of hundred dollars to educate a student, whereas America and other capitalist countries spent close to $10,000 per year to teach a student. Its literacy rate and graduating result for high school are also higher than what we see in America. However, one of its flaws was that it required excellent students to tutor and watch over bad ones so that all students could move ahead together. For Viet, this was a major inconvenience, because he could not move ahead fast enough to acquire new knowledge. Besides, if someone does not want to learn and chooses instead to goof around in school, a good tutor cannot make the person enjoy learning and get good grades. Indeed, the whole concept of "no child left behind" being promoted in the American education system was implemented by the Communists. Unfortunately, students like Viet did not see the true value in the concept and found it a drag for learning and advancement.

Although the Communists tried to promote this concept in its education system, it still allowed a little bit of competition in school and some achievement recognition for every semester. Viet loved that aspect and found it to be the main source of excitement for his schooling. He was a bright and hard-working student and enjoyed competing in school in class and on the field. He received various awards every semester during his entire high school career. As far as his grades and knowledge were concerned, he could become a doctor, engineer, teacher, or anything he wanted. However, like many young people, he was not quite sure what he wanted to do with his life yet. He liked to build things and figure out how things work. Naturally, he might want to be an engineer. That way, he could help rebuild his country after the devastating war. On the other hand, he loved to ease the pains and heal the wounds of others. That means he could be a doctor and help all the brokenness and suffering he had seen on the streets of Saigon.

Some people figure out their life mission by continuing with what they have enjoyed doing all their lives. Others make a career out of a certain trade because it produces money for them. However, some get into a business because it brings them fame, prestige, or notoriety. All these things were appealing to a young person like Viet. Moreover, coming from a poor and shattered country like Viet Nam, all the rewards and career opportunities were like manna from Heaven for him. For Viet, prestige and money were nice compensation. But, he witnessed how they could not bring true happiness, especially after the Viet Nam War. His own father had both prestige and money in his position in National Security for South Viet Nam. Unfortunately, the Communists invaded the South and everything he achieved vanished. Other South Vietnamese suffered the same fate as they were imprisoned and exiled. His own family had to burn paper currency as fuel to cook their meals and survive day by day after the war.

The Communists also ceased property ownership and took material possessions from the public as they got control of the country and turned many lives upside down. Viet could try to become a doctor, an engineer, or someone who sought fame, prestige, money, material possessions, and a good career opportunity. But, he believed all these things would not bring him true happiness and peace in his heart based on everything he saw at the end of the war. They were just empty promises and vain allurements that would not give him reasons to wake up every day under the Communist system. So, he continued to discern in prayer and search further to see what God would call him to do.

As Viet continued his search for his life's mission, his father was still in a reeducation camp. He did not know when his father would be released. He had to take charge of his family and tried to take care of his family while still going to school full-time. He had to babysit, change diapers, bathe, and feed his two younger sisters while his mother went to work as a seamstress to make ends meet for his family. He tried to get supplies from the government-run stores and outdoor market for his family daily. To accomplish that task, he learned to bargain and get a good deal and great products at all those outlets. He also needed to pay attention to the daily and weekly announcements from the local authorities regarding when certain consumer items such as rice, meat, fish, sugar, salt, clothes, fabric, household products, and other necessities might be sold. Once he knew the time information, he had to get to the stores early, stand in long lines for over an hour, and hopefully get most of the products released by the government for his household. Sometimes, he needed to come back to the stores more than once and hope to get whatever the public did not want to buy. He used a bicycle to transport or carried on his shoulder eighty-kilogram bags of rice and other heavy items over a mile to his home. It was not unusual to see things break apart or pour out all over the road. Viet had experienced one of his bags of rice tear open in the middle of the road or his watermelons roll off his bike and burst open several times. His family was not happy about these accidents, and he had an earful of lectures when he got home.

Besides getting daily supplies from the government-run stores and outdoor markets, Viet also had to get water from the neighborhood well and collect rainwater in his family's water basin. He did not know when that well was dug and who drilled it. But, it had always been there since he was a baby. He used to play around there with his neighborhood friends on hot days and bathe with them to cool off. He also tried to collect rain water in his family's water basin, which was about twelve meters deep by twelve meters wide by twelve meters long. Rain water was usually clear and tasted better than well water. Unfortunately, there were warnings about acid rain and other contaminations from climate pollution.

Viet recalled the Chernobyl nuclear reactor accident in the Ukraine and how its toxic, deadly cloud affected the rain water. But, he did not have much choice and had to keep collecting rain water for survival even though there was a big risk of cancer and other illnesses from drinking it. His situation was like people who lived close to the

624 | 9781457558160 | 624

Location: B25

VOM.IXY

Title:	Living For Higher Purpose: Story of a City Boy Who Survived the Vietnam War by Living for Jesus and Others
Cond:	Good
User:	vo_list
Station:	Workstation-01
Date:	2021-10-11 20:27:36 (UTC)
Account:	Veteran-Outsource
Orig Loc:	B25
mSKU:	VOM.IXY
Seq#:	624
unit_id:	3148163
width:	0.44 in
rank:	3,205,504

delist unit# 3148163

XXXXX

regions where Agent Orange was used in the Viet Nam War. Its consequences included all sorts of illnesses, such as cancers and birth defects. He saw many horrible- looking babies and early deaths as the living witness of the terrible war. Because of many hidden dangers in the water, Viet and his countrymen usually boiled their water and collected it in crystal bottles for later use. He also had to clean up the house, do laundry, cook meals, and do everything possible to take care of and protect his family as the man of the house since the time he was ten years old.

He remembered the first time he had to cook rice. He did not know how much water to pour in the pot and how to manage the fire. He ended up with a pot of rice with three layers. The top layer was undercooked, the middle layer was half-cooked, and the bottom layer was badly burned. His cooking skills improved over time and became a good asset for him in the future. He also had to fend off dangerous things such as snakes, poisonous spiders, scorpions, roaches, and big rats. He had never seen such a big rat in his home before, but once he had to deal with one particular rat with big teeth and a bad attitude. He was only twelve years old at the time, and his mother and sisters were screaming at the sight of that rat. He had to put aside all the fear, catch it by the tail, and quickly swing it into a cage before it had a chance to bite his tiny hand.

These are just a couple of examples of how Viet needed to take care and protect his family at all costs. He never shied away from anything that might help make the life of his family and others a little better. He also took on some part-time jobs such as assembling small tiles to create a sheet of various patterns, making carrying bags, and sewing sweaters and clothes. He tried to earn some income and help his family besides going to school full time. At the same time, he maintained good grades and stayed at the top of his class.

Viet looked back on this period of his life and realized that he picked up lots of important virtues such as working hard, dedication, sacrifice, caring, kindness, generosity, courage, humility, hope, and resilience, all of which would serve him well in the future. He also learned that he could do anything if he put his mind to it. He would not let anything hold him back or make him feel shy about reaching out to help others.

He slowly realized that his life was about making a difference in the lives of others. He could not live simply for himself and keep

God's blessings all to himself. The idea of living for others or a higher purpose made Viet feel alive and useful. He could not keep on living for himself and feel alone in the vast Universe. His life from that moment forward would be about helping others, especially his family. He felt happy and honored to be the hero of his family, even though he had to work extremely hard and make many personal sacrifices for it.

Despite his hard work and excellent grades in class, the Communist government let him know that he could not go on to college and achieve his dream because his father worked for the former regime. Like many governments, the Communists were quite vengeful and continued to punish the next generation because of the sins of its forefathers. Moreover, they were afraid that if the children of the former regime officials succeeded, they might sabotage and overturn them. Viet soon realized that he would never have a chance to achieve his dream or do anything good with his life under the Communist government despite his good grades and excellent work ethic. He had to do something drastic if he would like his life to have a meaning and fully blossom.

While trying to contemplate what he would do next, Viet decided to take a long trip to visit one of his uncles and his family in the countryside one summer. They lived about a hundred kilometers southwest of Saigon city. Viet had to take a public bus and switch to a different one three times before he arrived at his uncle's home. This was his first long trip away from home all by himself. He also had not seen this uncle since the collapse of Saigon. He felt a bit nervous and anxious. He did not know this was a dry run for his upcoming trips as he tried to search for freedom and a new world. On the day before his trip, he packed his clothes, personal hygiene products, and some gifts for his uncle. The next morning, he woke up before sunrise, had a quick breakfast with his family, and said goodbye to them before heading out to a bus stop near his home.

As he waited for his bus to come, he remembered how he was tricked and lost his other uncle's bicycle. He also heard about many cases of pickpocketing, robbing at knife point, and kidnapping at public bus stops. He became a bit worried and fearful waiting for the bus all by himself. At that moment, he remembered the advice of his grandparents, who taught him to bring his concerns to God in prayer and ask God for help. That was exactly what Viet did, and he no longer felt scared or alone. He believed that God and his grandparents were right there with him. After a little over half an hour of waiting, his bus finally arrived, and he hopped onto the crowded public vehicle. Everyone was packed tight like sardines on this dilapidated bus. There were also poultry and people sitting on the roof of the bus and hanging on to the back. The bus used steam power to run its engine by burning coal to heat up the water. An assistant on the bus had to tend the fire during the journey and sparks flew out all over the road. During this several-hour-long trip, the bus stopped several times along the highway to refill its water and coal. Viet saw lots of rice fields and farmland on both sides of the highway. At these short stops, street vendors ran up to the bus trying to sell foods, snacks, drinks, and some knickknacks to the bus riders. This was something Viet never saw before and found it a bit fascinating. After a few bus exchanges, he finally arrived at his uncle's village. Then, he had to walk a kilometer on a small dirt road and take a canoe down a river to get to his uncle's home.

His uncle and the entire family came out to greet him. Viet never met everyone before and had to learn their names in a hurry. He finally got settled in and had his first dinner with the household. Nothing was different at this meal with his uncle's family compared to Viet's family, as everyone said grace and gave thanks together for the food. The only difference was that they sat on the dirt floor for the meal and used a kerosene lamp to light the house in place of electric lights like the city folks would do. There was no television or radio. It was Viet's first experience being away from civilization and modern conveniences. The whole village looked quite dark at night as each home was lit up with a couple of kerosene lamps or some burning candles. Viet felt a bit uneasy as if he just landed on some far away planet. But, he quickly fell asleep in this dark and quiet village after a long day. He was also grateful that he left behind in the city all the noises of traffic, screaming neighbors, street vendors, and fighting animals. Everything seemed a bit more calm and slower in village life.

Viet woke up the next morning and was introduced to the life routine of a farmer. He was first led to the chicken coop and poultry pen, where he saw a bunch of chickens and ducks. There were some baby chicks and ducklings following them. He also spotted some fighting roosters in the coop. In Asian culture, rooster fighting and betting is one of the traditions that people enjoy and follow religiously. A person can find big crowds on the streets watching roosters fight every day. Viet would love to have one fighting rooster at his home in Saigon, even though he did not know anything about this game or gambling. Next, he was shown to the pig pen where his uncle had half a dozen pigs and their piglets. They quickly moved on to a group of cattle-like cows and buffaloes being kept a little further away from the house. Viet had never seen these domestic, but magnificent, creatures in person. He felt a bit nervous when he approached the water buffaloes, with their sharp, intimidating horns. His relatives convinced him that all the farm animals, including the mean water buffaloes, were harmless. He helped them feed those animals on his first morning in the countryside. Before long, they were ready to head home for lunch. Once again, Viet found it a bit strange to sit on the dirt floor and have a meal with his uncle's family instead of sitting on chairs and benches at a table as he used to do at home. But, it felt a bit more homey and friendly the way his uncle's family sat and shared meals with one another.

Like the city life, everything shut down in the village after lunch for a couple of hours so that everyone could take a nap. This custom was adopted and passed on during the French occupation. Viet Nam was a French colony for more than two hundred years and was very much influenced by French and European customs. One of those customs was taking a siesta after lunch. This custom was difficult for young kids like Viet to carry out daily. Most kids enjoy playing or doing something fun instead of napping. Sleeping is sometimes considered a wonderful hobby that dead people enjoy! But, Viet could not resist the gentle breeze and the quiet atmosphere of the countryside, and he slowly drifted into a snooze, just like everyone else. After his nap, his cousins took him out to the pond about a hundred yards behind the house. They raised fish and shrimp in that pond to eat and sell to the public. They showed him how to feed and harvest them when the right time came. They took Viet out a bit further to a giant field where they planted rice and other vegetables.

As Viet looked toward the end of the field, he spotted three resilient trees that had survived many wars and provided great resources for the native folks over the years. They were coconut, banana, and bamboo trees. Native people have produced wonderful dishes and drinks out of a coconut and made good use of the coconut tree for various household items. The same thing was true for the banana tree. Besides harvesting the bananas, native people used the banana buds to cook with fish and make a delicious soup. They cut down the banana leaves to wrap rice cakes and use them as a serving plate for food vendors. Children used the trunk of a banana tree as a floating device to help them learn how to swim. Finally, bamboo trees had been used to make long-lasting household products, even a floating barge. Native people also used bamboo roots for some delicious meals. Viet's cousins even showed him how to make a great fishing rod out of a bamboo branch. With that great tool ready, they promised to take him out for a fishing trip after dinner. Viet could not wait.

Viet went home for dinner with his uncle's family after a productive day and eagerly looked forward to the fishing trip as he counted down the minutes before sunset. Around nine o'clock, everything looked pitch dark, and his cousins called him to pack their fishing gear for a fishing adventure with some neighborhood kids. Their fishing rods and spears were all made of bamboo trees. With a few lanterns and a rickety boat, they set out to patrol their river banks and searched for fish. It was amazing to see how these professional fishermen read the signs in the river to know where the fish were. After a few hours going down the river, the group caught a whole bunch of fish with its spears and fishing rods and soon called it a night. Viet had a lot of fun and picked up all sorts of fishing tricks that evening. He continued to hang around his uncle's house for several more days before that fun week in the countryside ended.

As Viet was getting ready to head home on Monday morning, his uncle surprised him with gifts to take home to the city. He sent Viet home with a fighting rooster and a couple of hens and ducks. He knew how Viet liked the rooster and did not hesitate to give him that valuable treasure from his farm. He was pleasantly surprised and humbled by his uncle's generosity and kindness. He left his uncle's home with a delightful heart and tearful eyes. The trip to the countryside was not just a vacation but also a wonderful learning experience and an eye-opening revelation for Viet for several reasons.

First, he could not believe the genuine love and the boundless generosity that his uncle's family showed him. Although they had a little bit of land and some cattle and poultry, they were not rich at all. They barely made a living and survived from one day to the next. But, they did not hesitate to give Viet anything he liked. For them, human relationships meant more than any worldly possessions. That rightful thinking enabled them to open their home and hearts to Viet or anyone else without any hesitation. They taught Viet to be generous and learn to share God's blessings for him with others. Moreover, they taught Viet that there was something greater than worldly possessions in this life, namely, human relationships. They would rather sacrifice worldly possessions and gain relationships than accumulate material things and lose the valuable bond with other human beings.

Second, they showed Viet that a simple, honest lifestyle is better than a rich, dishonest one. That was why they were happy and comfortable with their country life. They did not have to cheat their neighbors or hurt others to make a living and get ahead. Perhaps, they had found the hidden formula for happiness for human beings living on earth. One thing Viet knew for sure about his uncle's family was that they were very content with their lifestyle in the countryside.

Finally, they taught Viet to trust in God by putting all their worries in God's hands after they worked hard and made wise choices. While city and modern folks might mock believers or not take their faith seriously, Viet's uncle had a strong and humble relationship with God. He relied on God to bless him with good weather for his field and harvest.

Viet's trip to visit his uncle's house helped him reconnect with some of his relatives. But, it also opened his eyes to new virtues and different perspectives. The love and generosity that his uncle showed him was unforgettable and transforming. It moved him to think about a career or vocation that would make a difference in the life of others by sharing with them the love and Good News of Jesus Christ. Viet was also challenged not to be selfish and keep God's blessings all to himself. He needed to share God's blessings with others and learn to help others as much as possible. That is how he could find true happiness and a fulfilling mission for his life. If he could learn to put the welfare of others and the mission of his Lord Jesus before himself, he would always be content with his life and have reasons to live another day.

Chapter 6

Searching for Freedom beyond the Borders

Around his sophomore year in high school, Viet collected sufficient information from the Communist authorities and other sources to learn that the children of the former regime officials would be denied a higher education or other prominent career in their new world order. Viet, the son of the former National Security official of South Viet Nam, soon realized that his life with the Communists would eventually come to a dead end despite his hard work and top performance in all his school years. Also around this time, his father thankfully was released from the reeducation camp. Everyone was not sure if he would ever be reunited with the whole family again and had slowly given up hope of seeing him alive.

Suddenly one early evening, he showed up out of nowhere at the door with a duffle bag. The whole family could not believe their eyes and were incredulous at what they saw in front of them. Even some of the neighbors were surprised to see Viet's father and asked his family if he was truly released from the camp. This must be how the early disciples felt when they saw the risen Christ. They were downcast and not sure if they would ever see their Lord Jesus again. Suddenly, he showed up in their midst despite the locked doors. The Gospels said that the disciples rejoiced when they saw the Lord. Viet knew exactly how they felt to see a lost member of one's family again. He shared their joy and excitement. This was indeed a miracle! This is what an Easter miracle would do to a person. It was more than winning the grand prize of Publisher's Clearing House!

Despite their original surprise, everyone was happy to see Viet's father again. Soon he had to report to the local authorities. He was also required to attend weekly meetings with them and jump through other hoops of the legal system as he tried to assimilate back into society and civilian life. After about a year of putting up with the harassment of the Communist authorities, Viet's father decided to sneak out of the country. He thought that by detaching himself from his family, the authorities would leave his family alone and no longer have any reason to give them a hard time.

In his quest to escape the country, he had many failed attempts and was arrested half a dozen of times. He was put in prison and tortured mercilessly every time to find out the ring leaders of the escaping group. Viet remembers that once his father was beaten badly and put into isolation while suffering horrible diarrhea. His entire family thought that he would die in prison that time. Fortunately, God kept on performing one miracle after another, and Viet's father got healthy again and was released shortly from prison.

Another opportunity came along for Viet's father to sneak out of Viet Nam by boat, and he was brave enough to go through with it after quite a few arrests and imprisonment. Thankfully, his wish and prayer to be freed from the yoke of the Communists was granted. He safely landed in a refugee camp in the Philippines after a couple of weeks floating at sea. He stayed in that camp for more than a year before being able to come to America. Having worked for South Viet Nam as an ally of the United States of America in the war against Russia and the Communists, Viet's father had no problem being granted political asylum in America. Viet's family thanked God for this great news and thought that the Communists would have no more reason to bother them and would let them live a peaceful life. Unfortunately, they continued to harass the family and focused on them a little more now that they knew Viet's father was in America.

Viet was approaching his senior year in high school and knew that his future with the Communists, including further education in college, would not go anywhere due to the "sins" his father had committed as an official of the former regime. He also learned from his father that there was a desperate need for religious vocation in America. The tough years after the Viet Nam War and with the Communists had helped Viet develop a strong faith and a desire to serve the Lord Jesus and his Church. By being a priest, he thought he could help the misfortunate and bring Jesus and His Good News to the broken world around him. These humble goals helped move Viet more quickly to decide to sneak out of Viet Nam like his father did to search for freedom and a bright future somewhere else. Still, it was very difficult for him to accept this serious decision to leave his family and friends behind. He was only seventeen and that decision would forever change his life.

Viet could only imagine how Joseph and Mary must have felt when they had to leave for Egypt with their son Jesus. They had to leave behind their family, friends, and all their possessions to avoid King Herod's persecution. They did not know when they might be able to come back and would have to assimilate into a new culture and way of life. Worse yet, they had to embark on a dangerous and long journey. They might lose their lives due to hunger, thirst, robbery, or other calamities. But, they knew that God was with them on that journey, and they had nothing to worry about.

Similarly, Viet was worried about the same things and did not want to risk his life for an idealistic purpose of serving the Lord Jesus and His Church as a priest. He learned that many folks lost their lives at sea or were stranded on a deserted island. Quite a few of the people who tried to sneak out of Viet Nam were arrested and put in prison for years. Viet was torn and scared about the decision to leave his homeland for a strange and distant land. On one hand, the Communists would not allow him to have further education and succeed or build a future in their society. On the other hand, the trip was extremely dangerous and uncertain. Less than 20 percent were able to tell their story of heroic adventures evading the Communist's capture and surviving dangers at sea such as drowning, being attacked by pirates, and starvation. After much prayerful consideration, Viet decided to risk everything and embark on that dangerous trip for the sake of his future and desire for freedom.

Whether he was ready or not, the day quickly came upon Viet as his family convened to share with him the details of his secret trip out of Viet Nam. One weekend, Viet was pulled over to a sound-proof room in the house and told that his family paid someone to take him to a boat to sneak out of the country. He had so many questions that day about the trip before he would risk his life for it. Who was this person? Where did they find him? How could they trust him? Could he be an undercover official and work for the government? Will he or any of his family members be going with me? How much did they have to pay him for my trip? Where is he going to take me? Is there a boat waiting for me some place? Is the boat sturdy enough for the rough sea and long voyage? How would I get to the boat? What is the total plan for the trip? How many people will there be on this trip? Who are the captain and the navigator? Will there be enough food, drink, and fuel for a long voyage? Does he have any plan to get everyone out of jail if the authorities catch us? Those were some of the questions Viet had about the trip. But, all he could think about at that moment was that this dangerous trip really happens now.

He began to have second thoughts about it and feel sad about leaving his family and friends behind. He was not sure if he would ever see them again. He was also asked to keep the whole trip a secret and not to say farewell to many people except a few close family members. Otherwise, if the local authorities found out about it, everything would be spoiled and many people, including Viet, would be put in jail. It was difficult and sad for any young person like him to keep tight lips and leave his loved ones without saying proper goodbyes.

Meanwhile, some of Viet's friends and neighbors left the country openly under a program called the Orderly Departure Program (ODP). The United States government began this program not long after the Viet Nam War to respond to the aftermath of that war and the overwhelming number of refugees that tried to flee the Communists' persecution. Many refugees lost their lives at sea or during their journey as they tried to search for freedom and a new life. Anyone who made it to neighboring countries such as Malaysia, Singapore, the Philippines, Indonesia, and Thailand overfilled the refugee camps and caused concerns for the authorities. The United States government and the United Nations High Commissioner for Refugees (UNHCR) saw the refugee problem and developed programs like ODP to address this urgent issue. Under the terms of this program, anyone—refugee or current citizen of Viet Nam—who had a loved one living in the United States could be sponsored by that person. After having proper paperwork for a certain amount of time, on average a few years, could fly directly to the United States without having to flee the country illegally. This program also allowed any Vietnamese who helped find a missing American soldier, living or deceased, leave for the United States. Some of Viet's friends and neighbors qualified for this program and apparently could say goodbye openly to everyone before their departure.

That day for Viet's departure was finally here. Viet skipped school that morning, had a quick breakfast, said goodbye to some family members, and took a tricycle ride, an Asian form of Uber or a taxi ride in big cities like Saigon, with a small personal bag to meet with his guide at a secret bus station. Viet and his guide took a day-long public bus ride to a village far away from Saigon and near a river that led to the Pacific Ocean. It took them all day travelling on different buses and getting to their destination around dusk because they needed to lose any potential secret police who might have followed them. When it was pitch dark, Viet was led to a home from their last bus stop. Viet did not eat anything all day and now was given something to eat on the run. He was thankful for that food, much like God's people were as they hastily ate at the Passover Feast and went on the trip out of Egypt. Yet, he was nervous and unsure about what would be waiting ahead for him.

Without a minute to spare, Viet was moved to another house to hide with another group of people. This exodus took place on foot in the dark and went on for a while as they traveled in secret to a few more houses. The group steadily grew to a couple of dozen people. They were told that at about 1 am they would get onto a taxi boat to take them out to a bigger boat that would survive in the ocean. After waiting in some bushes along the river bank in complete darkness for a signal to enter a taxi boat, the group did not hear or see anything and began to get worried.

Still, the group remained in hiding for another hour or so, but everyone knew that something went horribly wrong. Suddenly, a messenger came to tell the group that its leader, who was supposed to bribe the local official and organize all the logistics and details of the escape trip, had been arrested. Either the official did not take the bribe or someone blew the whistle on him and turned him into the authority. Now, the whole group had better get out of there fast and find their way home before everyone was arrested. They were also cautioned that they would need to spread out and wait at different places to catch the bus back to the city. Otherwise, the whole group would create suspicion from local authorities and be rounded up for jail.

Although everyone was cold, hungry, and thirsty, that sudden bad news was enough to drive them out of the bushes and run for their lives. Like a bunch of disturbed ants, they all tried to get out of there as fast as they could.

Without a flashlight or any point of reference, Viet picked a route amidst darkness and ran as far away from the group as he could. He did not know where he was going, but he had to get out of that dangerous place. In some way, it was exactly how he felt while living under the control of the Communists. He knew that he had to search for a new life away from his current, prison-like living. He had to risk his own safety to go out into a world of darkness to find any ray of hope for his life. He ran and kept running in that dark night until he spotted the silhouette of a watch tower at the end of the horizon. But, as he looked down in front of him, he saw a large body of water—a swamp or pond. Viet tried to walk along side of it and hide himself behind tall grass and bushes. Unfortunately, the watch tower already spotted him.

All of a sudden, he heard gunshots and saw traces of fire rushing toward him amidst total darkness. Without any time to think, he jumped quickly into the water to duck and dodge the hissing and flying traces of fire. As his body was completely submerged under the cold water, he soon realized that those traces of fire were bullets. They were like the ones flying all over the place at the end of the Viet Nam War. He was in basic training with the Communists for a summer, but never experienced any live firing or real combat before. Now he was being shot at by his own government. Those were not warning shots. Those were killing shots, and they were aiming right at him. They wanted to kill him.

As those dark thoughts went on in his head, Viet's desire to live kicked in, and he began to move all his arms and legs to get himself to the surface. As soon as his face cleared the water, he could not wait to take in a breath of fresh air. He felt so alive after that breath and was so happy to stay alive. That breath of fresh air was like a sweet taste of freedom for Viet. It woke him up from his dark night of the soul and near-death experience. He began to cough out some water that he swallowed as he went down under the water. As soon as the last drop of water came out of his mouth, he realized that he was not a good swimmer. Only his sheer will and desire to live pushed him out of the cold, dark body of water and helped him take in the fresh air he needed to live.

In that cold, dark body of water, Viet experienced death and darkness. He was shot at and was almost drown. If either one of those misfortunes happened to him, his loved ones would never find him. He surely had a close encounter with death that night. Like his Savior Jesus and all baptized Christians, Viet had to go down into the water of baptism and experience death to his old way of life for him to find the resurrection and a new life in the risen Christ. He came out of that body of water that early morning a bit scared but much more confident in himself and trusting in divine help a bit more. He also felt that his ancestors and grandparents must have been there with him on that dangerous and scary night. Their prayers must have reached Heaven. God had heard and sent an angel to save him from the flying bullets and near drowning experience.

From that moment on, he knew he could not live with the Communists and continue to live like a prisoner with a death sentence or a walking dead man. He would have to risk everything, even his own life, to search for a life of freedom and hope. That night Viet passed the point of no return as far as his decision of sneaking out of the country was concerned. He was resolved to leave his birthplace by all possible means, and nothing could hold him back or change his mind about it.

However, there was no time for him to stop and sort those emerging thoughts. He was in extreme danger, and it was time for him to run from the exposed location and find a new hiding place. He decided to run away from the watch tower of the local authorities and hide in the field of the village. He decided to hide himself in one of the straw piles that the villagers left in the field after their harvest. From his hiding place, he heard many human conversations and dogs barking and saw spotlights. The entire field was completely quiet after the gun shots. Now, it became alive with human footsteps and loud exchanges. During his childhood, Viet used to play hide and seek with his friends every day. He knew how to find the best hiding place and had mastered the art of invisibility to his seekers. He did not know how beneficial this game would be for him in real life until this very moment. Now, he would have to make good use of those skills and hope to outplay the Communist authorities.

Viet assumed he made a good choice on this hiding location and settled in it with some prayers. The loud conversations and rustling noises came closer to him and he could feel the poking sound of the bayonets and sticks around his pile of straw. One of the bayonets came down very close to him and missed him by mere inches. He could hear this group of patrollers strategize and discuss where they should focus their search for the members of this botched escape group as they poked around his hiding location. They went up and down his pile of straw and lingered there for quite some time before deciding to move on. Meanwhile, Viet had to stop breathing and kept on praying for divine protection from those patrollers. His prayers apparently were answered as the search party moved on to other parts of the field and continued its hunt.

Viet heard their exchanges from a distance that they caught some folks from his group. He began to settle down for the rest of that scary night and tried to catch some shuteye before preparing for his next move. He quickly made his sleeping bed out of the straw and looked up at the clear sky full of bright stars as he laid down to spend his first night ever alone in the field. He had always been surrounded by his family since childhood, especially growing up in an Asian family. Unlike Western nuclear families, Asian families often have two or three generations living together under the same roof. On that cold night, Viet was all by himself and could relate to Baby Jesus and all the homeless as they had to face having no safe shelter for sleep. They had to use whatever was available for them to lay down their heads for some rest. Viet had to sleep with one eye open that scary night as he was aware of many dangerous creatures like poisonous snakes, scorpions, and other wild animals possibly lurking around the field looking for food.

The dawn of a new day could not come soon enough as Viet saw the first beautiful ray of sunshine coming up at the far end of the field. Although a new day would be coming for Viet, it did not mean that all his troubles were over. Now, he had to figure out how to get home and be reunited with his family in Saigon city. However, he first had to figure out which local folks did not collaborate with the Communists and wouldn't turn him in. He could not knock on the door of each home and ask if they had any connection with the Communists or sympathy for them or not. He had to use his instincts and signs around a house and some luck from above to get himself some help to the city. He saw some homes with the Communist flag of red background and one yellow star in the middle hanging outside. Those were clearly places where people were loyal to the Communists and he must stay away from them.

Others had a vehicle like a car or a motorcycle parked in front of them or were built a bit fancy. Viet recalled that, after the Communists took over the South, they took everything from people such as property, jewelry, gold, vehicles, and other possessions. Then, they all lived a fancy lifestyle while the rest of their people suffered daily. That was when Viet learned the truth about the whole idea of Communism and Socialism. It was simply a hoax and a disingenuous idea. Under that careful analysis, Viet considered any home with a fancy appearance as belonging to Communist officials, because only they could afford and have the right to those things. He would be better off avoiding those homes.

He almost gave up on the hope of finding a home that had no connection with the Communists and might lend him a helping hand. Then, God showed him an old, simple home with a statue of Mary near the front door. It must belong to a Catholic family. Viet remembered that most Catholics were usually very loyal to their faith and had tried to resist the Communists (who basically did not believe in God). He knew that he could trust this family and slowly approached the front door to knock on it. His hand was shaking as he extended it toward the door. He did the necessary analysis about the home, but he could be wrong and quickly arrested in less than a few minutes.

After a short wait, an elderly couple opened the door and wondered what Viet wanted. He quickly explained his situation and asked for some help to get back to Saigon after a failed escape trip and a hairy night. Surprisingly, the couple agreed to help and invited this young stranger into their home. They gave him something to eat and drink while letting him know that they already knew about his failed escape trip. News travels fast in towns and villages. The local authorities had already checked their home over night to see if they might have harbored fugitives of this trip. He was told that some people of his group were captured last night, while others were picked up at dawn when they asked for direction around town. They also shared with him that some of their family members were arrested for trying to sneak out of the country like Viet. Hence, they were not friends of the Communists at all. They warned him to be extra careful on catching the bus home. They gave him some money to get home and told him detailed instructions how to elude the authorities at checkpoints after a public announcement was sent out about his group. Viet lost money and everything when he was told to leave his belongings and run for his life after his group leader was arrested.

Viet saw the presence of his grandparents in the wisdom and kindness of this elderly couple. He was not led to that home by accident. His ancestors and Lord Jesus must have been with him throughout that horrific night and especially that crucial morning. Without the protection and guidance of his ancestors and Jesus, Viet would not have found that kind and loving couple in that dangerous place. He could easily pick the wrong home and be arrested immediately. Along with his family, that elderly couple helped Viet form the mission for his life, namely, he must live for Jesus and others to repay all the kindness and blessings he had received from people around him throughout the course of his life.

Viet managed to get back to Saigon safely on his own without any guide. But, he ran out of money at the last bus stop and had to walk home in the rain for more than ten miles. He did not know which way his home was. He was quite worried and completely understood how the Magi must have felt when the star disappeared, and they did not know how to get to Bethlehem. They were lost, confused, worried, and a bit scared. They automatically latched on to a local resident for help and guidance, namely, King Herod. But, what they did not realize was that Herod was a snake, a fox, and a devil in human form. It was like Little Red Riding Hood asking the wolf for help and getting herself in lots more trouble. Realizing this, Viet did not talk to any stranger, but knew that his loving God and beloved ancestors were always by his side to watch over him. With the guidance of his guardian angel, he made it home safely before dusk after a couple of hours walking. His family already knew the trip was a bust and was happy to welcome him home at the door entrance. Like the Prodigal Son returning home after a short absence, they gave him a good shower, a warm meal, and dry, clean clothes.

Viet had a good night's sleep in his own bed that night. However, his life was forever changed from that failed trip. He became a man and made lots of serious decisions on his own. He stared death in the face for the first time on that dark night in the swamp and would no longer be afraid of it like many people often would. He felt much confidence in himself and knew that his faithful ancestors and loving

God would always be by his side to protect and help him. As such, his life must be about a higher purpose, and he was able to make them proud after everything that had been done for him.

After that failed trip, Viet continued to sneak out half a dozen other times with the help of his family. They had to pay at least a couple of thousand dollars for each trip. They also got tricked and scammed by several dishonest folks. But, they never stopped supporting him and believing that he could do great things with his life outside of Viet Nam. As Viet looked back on his attempts to sneak out of Viet Nam, there was one more trip that was quite memorable. After many failed attempts, conventional wisdom told him to give up on his dream of searching for freedom and a new life. However, he never threw that dream away or let anything scare him from embarking on another trip again.

Viet's family realized his resolve and scraped together all its resources to find a new connection for him to take on a new trip. This time he had to travel further north to a village northeast of Saigon for his new adventure. He also learned that this village was very pro-Communist, and he would have to be extremely cautious compared to other locations before. Again, Viet had to say farewell to his family while pretending to live a normal life with his friends and neighbors. He attended school right up to the day of his departure and did other daily routines around home without arousing any suspicion from his friends and neighbors. Otherwise the local authorities would find out about the secret plot of escape and many people would be arrested.

Keeping a secret like this was harder to a teenager than one might imagine. Yet, with much practice, Viet mastered this skill, which might be useful for him in the future. He could hide his emotions and no one could tell what was really going on in his head. But, keeping a secret was not as difficult to him as saying goodbye to his loved ones. The day for his departure was finally upon him. As he was about to put on his clothes for this trip, his mother told him to put on a special pair of pants and a custom-made pair of shoes. As a seamstress herself, she knew everything about sewing and hid some US dollars in the pants around the waist. Other family members did the same with his shoes. Apparently, they did not want to see Viet get stranded in the middle of nowhere without any money. They also packed him some medicine to help with seasickness. After checking on all the necessary items for the trip and giving him their final instructions, his family bid him farewell and wished him the best.

Viet met up with his guide at a bus stop like he did with other trips before. He felt like he was an expert at this. His guide gave him instructions as usual. He told Viet not to make any direct contact with him in public, even though they were sitting or standing across each other. He warned Viet to be very aware of the surroundings to avoid any secret police trailing them as they hopped from one bus to the next. Their long trip took almost a whole day, but they finally arrived at the designated village. Viet then was transferred to a different guide who took him to a hiding home to be with other participants of the trip. Next, the group was brought to a taxi boat to join with half a dozen other groups at a bigger boat that could travel out in the ocean. Viet's taxi boat navigated through the dark night and the complex system of rivers of this tropical country for several hours before it arrived at its destination.

Suddenly, the engine was turned off and everyone was told to stay quiet as they waited for other taxi boats and the mother boat to join them. In total darkness and complete silence, they patiently waited. As Viet joined his boat mates in waiting for the mother boat, he could not help but think about the season of Advent that Christians are called to wait for their Savior and His second coming. They usually light the four Advent candles and try to keep vigil in prayers expecting that moment to come. Apparently, at Jesus' first coming, the whole world found itself deep asleep and missed the whole miraculous show. The only ones who witnessed that miraculous event were the shepherds. They had to stay awake to watch their sheep in the field. They were rewarded for staying alert by hearing the angels' announcement of that incredible event and were led to the Manger of the Savior. Taking note from that first Christmas, Christians have tried to stay awake and keep vigil in prayers for their Savior's second coming. Like these Christians, Viet tried to wait for that mother boat by staying awake with the help of prayer.

An hour went by, but there was no sign of that boat or other taxi boats. Signs of sunrise and daylight were showing up all around them. They could only sneak out in darkness, and those signs meant that their trip would soon be a bust. Something was wrong. But, they had no way to find out what it was. There were no cell phones or citizen band radios, or walkie-talkies to communicate that crucial information.

While everyone was confused and stranded in the middle of the river, a Coast Guard patrol boat spotted them and quickly arrested them. They all were put in a local prison without any due process or explanation about their future. Viet knew this moment would come someday as part of the risk of his escape trip. But, he could not believe he was finally arrested and had to face an uncertain future. He never did anything wrong to be put in jail, let alone prison, and now he was quite scared about life behind bars. He always managed to get home quickly to rejoin his friends in school after a failed trip. This arrest would certainly confirm his friends and neighbors' suspicion of his desire to escape his homeland. Worse yet, if he was kept in prison long enough, it might ruin his whole school year, and he would have to retake his entire junior year of high school. His prison record might even keep him from being eligible to attend college for sure.

While Viet was worrying about his good name and school eligibility status, he did not know half of the problems waiting ahead for him in prison. First, everything he had was taken away and he was strip-searched at the gate of the prison. One of the prison guards asked for his name and fingerprinted him. They also shaved his head against his will. Then, along with several boat mates, he was thrown into a crowded cell of more than a couple of dozen people. The cell leaders made him strip naked a second time in the front of the whole group and verbally harassed him. They did the same to all his boat mates. They wanted to rattle the new prisoners and see what they could get out of them. What they did not realize was that the prison guards and the local authorities already took everything. Perhaps this was a tactic that old prisoners used to intimidate and let the new prisoners know who oversaw the prison besides the guards.

Viet had never been in prison before and did not know anything about the prison culture. He was shocked and surprised by what he saw. But, he was smart enough to comply with the demands of the old prisoners. After all, it is a dog-eat-dog world, and prison is a miniature model of it. A couple of his boat mates were loud mouthed and defiant to the demands of the old prisoners. They were rubbed up and beaten badly; indeed, the prison guards saw the whole thing and did not intervene at all. Only later did Viet discover the identity of the old prisoners. They were murderers and street gang thugs. The local authorities basically threw the failed escapees and political dissidents into the same cells with common criminals without any regard. As far as the Communists were concerned, anyone who opposed them in any way was criminal. They did not care if a criminal was hurt or killed in the prison.

The first few hours in any prison cell are scary and harrowing, but the first few days in a Communist prison were pure hell for Viet. First, they fed prisoners only two meals a day with only rice and nothing else. Their rice not only looked bad but also tasted horrible. It was low-grade, discarded rice that one would use only to feed farm animals. Some prisoners helped cook the rice every day by dumping a fifty-kilogram bag into a huge cooking pan and using a garden shovel to stir it. That certainly was not quite appealing to Viet's appetite even though he was starving. Then again, this was not first-class cooking for royalty or a resort. He would have to eat anything presented to him if he wanted to survive this prison experience and make it home alive. First he would need some sort of bowl or container to hold the rice or any food provided.

The prison guards gave the new prisoners nothing except torture and misery. Viet's money and possessions were all taken away, and the only things he had left were his jacket, shirt, and pants. He had to exchange his jacket for a beat-up container and a spoon. Everyone lined up for some rice, and the line was quite long. There must have been a couple of hundred people. They used a big shovel to distribute the rice, but only a handful of it landed in each person's bowl or container. Viet brought his portion of the rice to a corner of the dining area and simply sat down staring at it for the longest time. His family was not rich, but he never had to eat bad rice without any vegetables or meat at all.

Like the prodigal son, Viet thought about the good food he used to have at home. He longed to have some of that food right now—a nice bowl of tasty rice with delicious meat and vegetables or a traditional bowl of noodles with roasted beef and fried onion. As he dreamed about the wonderful meal he used to have at home every day, he finally convinced himself to take the first bite and swallow it. As soon as it went past his throat, he started to throw up. The smell and taste of the rice was awful. It had a mixture of smoke and rotten egg.

He tried to chew it, but the rice seemed to have sand and dirt mixed with it. He never imagined he would have to eat horrible food like this. However, to help him keep up his strength and survive, he would need to finish his bowl of rice by swallowing one mouthful at a time. After that horrible meal, Viet could sympathize and relate to the poor and what they must go through each day with their food. They might not have enough food, or their food could be worse than what Viet just ate. They had to struggle to find food for their families every day. They do not know where their next meal might come from. Viet wondered if they could swallow the food that they found in the trash cans. As he thought about the plight of the poor and the horrible food he just experienced, tears rolled down his cheeks.

Before he could wipe away his tears, his name was called, and he was summoned to the Interrogation room. He learned that during the first hour after the new prisoners were admitted, the prison authority had already started to interrogate some of the important people of his group, including the owner of the taxi boat, the navigator, the mechanic, and so on to find out about the whole operation and its leadership. They were threatened, tortured, and beaten. Their screaming and loud cries could be heard throughout the prison camp. Viet could see his boat mates all had a worried and scared look on their faces. He tried to remain calm as he headed to that scary room. His ability to keep a secret in the past surely came in handy at this moment. It would not matter how horrible the Communist tactics of investigation might be; Viet was determined that he would not break his silence and reveal anything useful about the escape trip to the authorities. Besides, his family made all the arrangements for his trip, and he truly did not have any involvement in its planning at all. Moreover, Viet always counted on his God and his ancestors to give him wisdom and guidance in times of need like this. He called on them in prayer to come to his aid and give him the ability to make it through the interrogation and the prison experience. With that prayer, he was ready for his turn to go in for interrogation.

Viet had never endured an interrogation in his life. In fact, he was always an excellent student and never disappointed or caused his teachers to be mad at him. He had never been scolded by any teacher or called into the principal's office. After waiting outside the Interrogation room for a little bit, he was finally led into the room. There were a couple of guys standing in the corner of the room in soldier uniforms holding AK-47s. In the middle of the room was a small table with a chair on each side of it. They told Viet to sit down in one of the chairs. After several minutes of waiting, another uniformed man came in and sat in the other chair across him. He asked Viet's name, his home address, his parents' names, and his and their current occupations. Viet was coached to give fake names and a fake address before the trip if he ever found himself arrested. He memorized all that information and confidently gave it all to his interrogator without missing a beat. His interrogator was a seasoned law officer. He tried to trick Viet by asking him follow-up questions: "Are you sure this is the right information? Do you know that it's not right to lie to the officer of the law?" He paused briefly and continued, "If I find out that you lie to me, you'll be in a lot of trouble and possibly put in prison for a long time!"

The interrogator then switched to a different set of questions and wondered how much Viet might know about the trip. He tried to find out who organized the whole escape and who paid for Viet's trip. Viet clearly did not know anything about the whole trip. After repeating the same questions several times and rephrasing them in a variety of ways, the interrogator tried to convince Viet to spill out anything he knew about the trip, but Viet had nothing useful to offer him.

Realizing the current questioning was going nowhere, the interrogator once again changed his tactic and tried to sweet talk Viet. He promised Viet that he would let him out of prison and would allow him to go home early if he would tell him anything about the trip and make the bad guys pay for this crime instead of him. Again, Viet disappointed the officer and provided nothing useful. Out of frustration, he slammed the table and stood up. He walked around Viet and hit him upside his head while reminding him loudly that he was currently in prison and would stay there for a long time if he tried to hold back anything or anyone involved with the trip.

Then, he pointed to the soldiers holding an AK-47s and threatened Viet that they would hurt him and might even shoot him without anyone knowing about it. Viet had learned from his father who was held in a reeducation camp and other POWs about some horrible methods of interrogation the Communists conducted including waterboarding, sleep deprivation, electric shock, severe beating, food-and-drink deprivation, or complete isolation. But, Viet did not flinch and kept on coming to Jesus and his ancestors to give him strength and guidance to make it through this horrible session. After more than several hours of intense questioning and harassment, the officer finally let Viet go and reminded him that he was not done yet.

Viet returned to his prison cell completely exhausted, but not intimidated by the experience. Before he could catch some rest, he was summoned to go out to work in the field with other prisoners. They had to dig a trench for irrigation in the hot sun. The next day they had to break a huge granite boulder into small pieces so that the government could sell the smaller stones and make some money. The work for prisoners changed from day to day, and there was absolutely no rest for the weary. Before he knew it, Viet had already stayed in prison for a week and was slowly adjusting to his life in prison. He was forced to eat bad food, work nonstop, and sleep on a dirty floor. He also had to listen to vulgar language daily, deal with harassment and threats from other prisoners, and endure constant interrogation with the prison authorities.

He also learned to make friends with some prisoners, including rats and cockroaches. These creatures made their home in the prison and did everything as they pleased. They were the only thing that could experience freedom in the entire prison. At first, they grossed him out and made him cringe. Soon, however, he fed them some of his food and talked with them. That was how Viet stayed sane and dealt with his homesickness. He also had to deal with a rough population of prisoners that included rapists, robbers, and murderers. Having rats and cockroaches as his friends, he remained calm amidst a group of hardcore criminals. He also made friends with a couple of good prisoners who ended up behind the barbwire and tighter security of the prison because they also tried to sneak out of the country like Viet.

As Viet tried to get adjusted to his new life in prison, his prayer finally got answered. One day, he was told he was being released due to his young age. Viet quickly collected his belongings and gave them to some prisoner friends who were left behind. Although he might have left prison with empty hands, his heart was full of joy and hope. He could not wait to walk out of the prison gates and smell the air of freedom even though it was limited, imperfect freedom. He tried to forget the prison experience, but it always stuck with him like a bad prison haircut. The prison authorities wanted to punish and mark Viet and his boat mates for their failed escape trip by giving them a really ugly haircut. That way, the public would know that they just gotten out of prison.

Thankfully, Viet scraped together enough money from a few friends in prison to get a ticket for a bus trip back to Saigon City. He safely got on a bus and, during that bus trip home, a lot of things went through his mind. On one hand, he felt defeated and shook-up by the failed escape and horrible prison experience. He was also worried about being held back in the same grade for another year because he missed more than a week of classes. He had lots of tests and homework to catch up on when he got home. On the other hand, he had his first taste of life in a Communist prison and learned how difficult real life can be based on his week-long experience. He had to deal with the interrogation by the Communists and prison living. Against all odds, he survived the hellish week and triumphed over the power of darkness. He did not know what was waiting ahead for him. Perhaps the local authorities had already crossed his name off the list of residents at his home. Or, maybe, his capture might give him and his family lots of problems once they found out about his failed escape. No matter how his future might turn out, he knew one thing for sure: he had to keep searching for freedom and a new life beyond his native country. He had passed the point of no return in his desire to escape the oppressed living situation. He was no longer afraid of prison or death. He was willing to risk his life and everything he had to find a life of hope and freedom.

He finally got off the bus after a day-long trip. He was tired and hungry, but determined to get home even though he had no money left in his pockets. Like the last failed trip, he started to walk away from the bus station and any potential undercover Communist agents in the tropical rain while trying to figure out the right way home. He thought about the long journey out of Egypt that God's people had to walk with Moses. They had to undergo all sorts of weather conditions and did not know where they were heading. They had to face poisonous snakes, hunger, and thirst. The only one on whom they could count for help and guidance was God. Certainly, God did not disappoint them and came to their rescue time and again.

Like God's people, Viet found himself praying to his faithful God and calling to mind his ancestors for some much-needed help. They had always been his source of guidance and strength in difficult times. His conversation with them also made his long, tiresome trip seem much shorter. After almost two hours of walking in heavy rain and thunder and trying to figure out the right way, he made it home at last. That was, in some way, a miniature journey of his life with the Communists. He felt lost and overwhelmed by all the hurdles that the government created for him every day. He knocked on the door and his mother quickly came and opened it. His mother and family were happy and thankful to see him home safe and alive.

When she said goodbye to him last time, she was not sure if she would ever see him again. She had learned that his group had been arrested, but did not know how long he would be kept in prison. She celebrated her son's safe return, but did not call on her family to put a fine robe, a diamond ring, and a pair of fancy shoes on her lost-and-found son, nor did they slaughter a fatted calf for his safe return like the story of the Prodigal Son. But, the whole family was certainly thrilled and thankful to see him again. They celebrated his safe return with homemade soup, fried rice, and eggrolls for dinner.

Chapter 7

The Great Escape at Sea

After the small celebration and a good night's sleep, Viet returned to school and his regular life the next day. When he got to school that morning, his schoolmates and teachers were pleasantly surprised to see him back to the class with them. Since kindergarten, he had always been one of the top students in the class and popular among his classmates. He was smart, hardworking, responsible, respectful, kind, caring, friendly, and funny. He represented his class and school in many academic and sports competitions at high levels and won one award after another. He also tutored his underperforming classmates and volunteered to help his teachers with class duties and other errands around the school. He was an all-around good guy and a top-class student. Everyone knew that he was destined to accomplish great things; hence, they were not surprised to learn that he tried to sneak out of the country to secure a better future.

Unfortunately, his escape trip failed. They learned all of this because he missed classes for a week and had a bad prison haircut. They did not attempt to ask him about the trip, but they teased him with comments such as, "Nice haircut! Did you get it in the USA?" or "Nice vacation you got! Did you spend it in Hanoi Hilton?" or "How was the fishing trip? Did you catch any fish at all?" Viet simply smiled and deflected these comments by not responding to them. After these initial reactions to his first day back in the class, life seemed to get back to normal for Viet. Thankfully, the local authorities did not give him and his family any grief or trouble since his return from prison. Maybe they did not know anything about his escape trip or arrest.

A week went by and then another month ended. Viet finally settled in to his daily routines and began to live his normal life for several months. Suddenly, he was told that there would be a new opportunity for him to leave the country within a week. His family had paid in full and lost a lot money for him to sneak out of the country on the failed trips. They were not sure if they could afford another for him. Besides, if he got caught again this time, the authorities might keep him in prison for years, because he repeated the same offense within a short period of time. His family gathered whatever they had and borrowed the rest of the money from their relatives to pay for one more trip for Viet. They were determined to support his dream of searching for freedom and a new life.

The trip was all paid for. Viet was told that his trip would be the next morning, and he had to pack quickly. That night, Viet's neighborhood lost electricity and darkness filled it. This phenomenon happened without any public notice four or five days a week, and it often lasted more than 24 hours. At first, it was just a public nuisance, but over time it had become a fact of life. The authorities told the public that they had to cut electricity to save resources. Viet could not hold back his tears as he said goodbye to his mother, siblings, grandparents, aunts, uncles, and other family members that dark night. Under the dimming light of a kerosene-burning lamp, his family prayed over him and sent with him their best wishes.

Unlike other farewell occasions, Viet felt that this time was a bit different and it might be the last time he would see them in person. His past experiences and gut feeling told him that this trip would be his final and successful one. He instinctually knew that he would not see them again in this life until they see each other in Heaven.

He remembered well that exact feeling as he said farewell to one of his aunts who came to visit his family from the North and had some children who were high-ranking Communist officials. During the Viet Nam War, the Communists recruited them to serve in their army for the North, whereas Viet's father and other men in the South were drafted to serve on the other side with the Americans. This war was truly a civil war because families were divided and fought one another. His family had some reservations and concerns about this aunt and her visit. They did not know if she would turn in the family to the Communists or fabricate a reason to gain favor with the authorities. Viet was not sure if he should say goodbye to her and risk exposing the whole trip. In the end, he decided to treat her as a family member and told her that he was going on a dangerous escape trip that night. She thanked him for letting her know about it, wished him a safe trip, and told him to come back to see her someday. Both began to cry as they shook each other's hands. Viet could not imagine he would receive such a warm and caring reaction from her. He thanked her for her prayers and support and promised to return to visit her in the future. He learned later that not too long after that farewell, she passed away. Viet completed his farewell tour with his family around 9 pm and was ready to sneak out to a designated meeting location under the cover of darkness to avoid being detected by his neighbors and the local authorities.

He met his guide right on time at a secret location and went to a house close to a bus stop for quick shuteye before catching a bus early the next morning. Again, it took Viet, his guide, and a few companions a whole day to ride the bus to a secret location southeast of Saigon near a river leading to the ocean. They also had to ride around in a couple of buses to shake any secret police. They also rode additional buses to kill time and wait until dusk to board a taxi boat that would take them to a bigger boat worthy of ocean travel. Everything went smoothly as planned, and everyone stumbled in the dark onto a taxi boat waiting for them on a river bank.

Viet was quite impressed with everything he had seen so far about this group of organizers based on his experience and knew that they were not scammers. After everyone boarded, the boat took off in the dark as everyone hunkered down below the boat deck. Then, the engine was suddenly shut off and the crew switched to their oars to move the boat quietly down the river. Everyone in the boat could hear the oars beating against the water. The boat moved quietly in the dark. Suddenly, the captain whispered down the boat deck and ordered everyone to remain absolutely silent as they passed through a Coast Guard checkpoint.

Suddenly, a baby burst out crying. It not only surprised everyone, but also made everyone on the boat mad as they tried to quiet the baby. "Make it stop! Or, they'll hear it, and we all will be arrested!" Everyone could not believe that someone would bring a baby on a dangerous trip like this. The mother apparently could not quiet her baby. The baby cried for several minutes, which seemed like forever. They could not cover the baby's mouth like they do in some movies to muffle its crying. After some quick prayers and encouragement to the mother to get the baby to stop crying, the entire boat managed to stay quiet for a while as it passed through the Coast Guard checkpoint.

During the commotion, everyone thought the boat would be discovered, and everyone would be arrested. Thankfully, it passed the checkpoint safely to join other taxi boats. Everyone hopped on the mother boat before heading out to the ocean together. That was the first miracle that Viet experienced and saw how the divine power and the protection of his ancestors would be at work throughout the trip. The mother boat was supposed to be bigger than the taxi boat, but it did not feel like that as everyone was sitting knee-to-knee and crammed under the deck. Although it felt uncomfortable in the boat, Viet instinctually felt hopeful that this trip would be successful. He would forever leave behind his old life under the yoke of the Communist government and begin a new one full of freedom and opportunities. But, he was not clear from all dangers and difficulties yet. This was just the beginning of a long, treacherous, and unforgettable voyage that he would remember for the rest of his life.

The boat dodged and maneuvered through checkpoints and Coast Guard patrol boats all night long. Viet found himself, along with his boat mates, sleeping through the whole thing. At one point, he heard someone ask the captain what was beneath the boat deck, and he responded that there were just some fish. The captain had surrounded us with smelly fish. But, he also bribed that patrol boat with some money before our whole boat was checked out and everyone arrested. Viet saw the patrol boat leave from the corner of his sleepy eyes, and his boat continued on its way. He looked through the cracks of the boat deck and saw some scattered lights that were slowly fading away toward the end of the horizon on a dark night as his boat moved forward into unknown territory. He breathed a sigh of relief and soon passed out from a long, difficult day of traveling and avoiding the Communist authorities.

But, this was not the end of his journey by any means. Rather, it was just the beginning of a long saga that would allow him encounter the risen Christ Jesus and experience countless miracles. His loving God let him see His mighty power like he did Jonah and God's people in their flight to the land of the free. Jonah apparently wanted to be freed from God's mission for him and ran away in search of his freedom. But, God caught up with him during his sea voyage and saved him from a destructive storm and an apparent death by embracing him in the belly of a whale. Jonah thought he could find freedom away from God. But, he found that only in God would he have true freedom and purpose for his life. Meanwhile, God's people tried to flee from their yoke of slavery in Egypt, but encountered challenges along the way, including the Egyptian army chasing them. Fortunately, they asked Moses to appeal to their God and they experienced one miracle after another throughout their journey to the free and Promised Land. God opened the sea to let them pass through safely, while using it as the graveyard against their enemies. God continued to watch over them, provide them with food and drink, and bring them healing and guidance throughout their long, treacherous journey. They would never forget that journey and the miracles that their God performed for them.

Viet did not know how long he slept, but the next thing he saw was the beautiful sunrise at the end of the blue water horizon. Those rays of sunlight represented rays of hope and freedom that Viet had dreamed about for the last decade. The gorgeous sunrise put an end to Viet's nightmare since Saigon collapsed and opened a new life of wonderful dreams and great promises. As he was taking in the beautiful sunrise, the boat captain called for everyone's attention and began to make an important announcement. He congratulated everyone for a successful escape from the Communist government and said they were currently in international water. What that meant was that the Communists could no longer arrest them, and they could count on other countries to rescue them. That might be true in theory, but in reality, the Communists and their allies could still catch them and put them in prison without any legal appeal process. The Communist pact still existed, and it included the Soviet Union, East Germany, Poland, Czechoslovakia, Romania, Cuba, China, North Korea, and others. The boat captain said they had some water, rice, and coconuts on the boat. They also had enough fuel to survive at sea for a week. Unfortunately, most of their food, water, and fuel were stolen or lost during the transition to the mother boat. Viet could feel his heart sink after hearing such bad news. He could not believe his long, dangerous journey started out like that. He needed all the help he could get from his loving God and encouragement from his ancestors to survive this trip.

While Viet was still processing the bad news, the boat captain continued his update of the boat situation. He told them they had an excellent engine mechanic and a good boat navigator, but none of them had ever made a long trip out into the ocean like this before. He also warned them about pirates from some horror stories that other escapees had encountered and wrote to tell about them. He asked all the men and boys to fight the pirates to the death, and warned the women and girls that they could be raped and killed. Viet knew martial arts, but he would be no match to the pirates' big guns. Besides, he might not have any strength with lack of food and drink and bad seasickness. The boat captain continued to run through all the worst-case scenarios and prepare his boat mates on how to deal with them. If their boat capsized, he suggested that everyone grab an empty fuel can or some floating device and try to hang on to it until help comes. His thorough preparation and important announcements surely got the entire boat ready for what might be coming, but it put a lump of coal in everyone's throat. Furthermore, it officially ended their big celebration of making it out of Viet Nam without being caught.

Anyone who ever dared to escape Viet Nam was given these statistics about the success or failure of the escapees: 50 to 60 percent of them would be caught by an authority, and 20 to 30 percent of them would be killed in the ocean or go missing without a trace due to drowning, piracy, or being stuck in a refugee camp or on some island for years. Less than 10 percent succeeded and made it safely to a refugee camp and then moved to a host country. Viet knew these statistics by heart and the odds of him being alive and surviving his treacherous trip were very low. He also realized that the Communist authorities usually loosened their tight grip of patrolling the coastal region around the end of the year, namely, November and December. These two months were often full of typhoons and dangerous sea conditions. The authorities did not want to risk their lives under those conditions. If anyone wanted to take on that risk and try to sneak out under those conditions, he or she was welcome to do so without any sympathy of the authorities.

Viet now found himself with other boat mates taking their trip in the middle of November under hostile, dangerous sea conditions. He recalled many drowning cases in the Saigon area in which the victims' bodies were carried by the ocean tide and dumped. He recalled one infamous case when more than a few dozen bodies drifted onto the beach of a five-star resort. That created a big commotion for the whole neighborhood. He and many neighbors went to check out the gruesome scene at the mortuary, where dead bodies filled it to capacity. All the bodies were dark, smelly, and ballooned with water due to saturation. Viet never forgot that gruesome scene, and now the same possibility of being drowned might be facing him.

After telling the whole boat about the impending dangers facing them, the boat captain pulled the tarp off the boat deck and let everyone enjoy the bright sun and breathe in fresh air. Having to squat knee-to-knee below deck for one night and one day not only caused everyone to cramp up, but also made many people nauseous. Apparently, tar was used to seal many fishing boats. The potent mixture of tar and the burning diesel fuel of the engine created a horrible, sickening smell on a hot day. It was worse than the smell of a newly constructed asphalt road on a scorching summer day. Certainly, the smell of dead fish in the boat did not help the boat's condition either. Adding to the nauseating smell, the constant bombardment of the waves made everyone feel dizzy and seasick.

Viet tried to eat some cooked rice that was passed out to everyone on the boat, but ended up vomiting everything out. He slowly felt dehydrated and wished to drink lots of water. But, all he was given was a small sip from the cap of a water bottle. He was told they had to conserve the water and was given only two sips a day. The hot sun and the ocean water that he used to enjoy on the beach now had become a problem for him. The ocean's salt water in the hot sun makes one's skin dry and leads quickly to dehydration.

Like God's people being stranded in the desert, Viet wondered if he made a mistake by leaving his safe shelter in Viet Nam in exchange for a place in a rickety boat floating dangerously in the ocean and lacking necessities. He began to fantasize about all the delicious food and ice-cold drinks he could have at home. He wished he could enjoy his favorite native foods like eggrolls, pho (noodles with beef), watermelon, and so on. Or, he could have some refreshing drink like soybean milk or cold tropical juice. He remembered some family gatherings that his grandparents put together for his relatives and cousins on big holidays such as Christmas, Lunar New Year, and ancestors' anniversaries. At these events, there were all kinds of food and lots of it. Everyone could eat to one's heart content and enjoy each other's company and stories. Viet particularly loved the play time with his cousins and the variety of games they played to keep themselves entertained, including hide and seek, hop-scotch, rope jumping, and so on.

As Viet reminisced of the good old days at home with his family and all the good food and drink he could enjoy, he was reminded of a home recipe that could put an end to his seasickness problem. Once again, his ancestors taught him to use ginger as a traditional remedy for seasickness, dizziness, and other stomach problems. Unfortunately, he did not have any ginger available to help him stop vomiting. All he had with him was prayer, which was his connection to his ancestors and a powerful source of help in times of need. He started praying for divine help to make him feel better from all the throwing up. As the sun rained down its warm sunlight, he gradually dozed off and tried to get some rest from his rough first day at sea. When he woke up, he overheard the boat captain talking about his navigation plan with some folks on the boat. Apparently, they wanted to do two things: head southeast to get to one of the refugee camps in Malaysia, Indonesia, the Philippines, or Singapore and at the same time try to avoid the Communist pact countries and pirate ships. Later, reality showed them that they had failed miserably on both these goals.

On this first clear, sunny day at sea, everyone could see the entire horizon and the surroundings as far as the eye could see. Everyone took turns scanning the horizon and was anxious to find something that looked like the shape of a ship in the distance to bring them hope for salvation. But, for hours, they did not see anything around them. When they were about to give up on any hope of finding anything on that vast ocean, they spotted the first ship on the distant horizon. Their first instinct was try to rush toward it. Fortunately, some careful folks in the group advised the captain to check it out first through the binoculars to see if the ship was friend or foe. The ships they needed to avoid were those that belonged to pirates and Communist countries. The Communist Eastern block was still active, and its ships would pull the boat back to Viet Nam, where everyone would be imprisoned indefinitely.

The ship was too far off for the boat captain to make out to which country it belonged. The group decided to take a chance and tried to rush to it for a closer look. Although the ship was within their sight, they were miles apart from it. It took a while to close the distance with the ship. When they got to the location that the ship was spotted, it was already gone. The boat's occupants continued to do this—search the horizon for a ship and run to it—for the entire afternoon, but ended the day empty-handed. Before long, evening came, and they faced their first night at sea. All signs—dark clouds and a muggy day—pointed to a rainy evening. But, they did not know how stormy and scary the night would turn out to be. In fact, some were looking forward to the rain to get some water and much-needed relief from the oppressive heat of a hot day.

Anticipating a stormy night, the captain put everyone all back under the deck and covered them with the tarp. Everyone was back to the uncomfortable position of squatting knee-to-knee and being packed like sardines next to each other at the bottom of the boat. Everything was dark, and all Viet could see through the open cracks and small holes in the deck was the bright stars and beautiful constellations in the dark sky. Viet could not imagine how beautiful the entire sky—part of God's magnificent creation—looked that night, but he often took it for granted while on land. This night brought back a similar experience for him when his neighborhood lost electricity for more than a day. His family hung out on the front porch or in the backyard enjoying star gazing and sharing family stories. Viet missed that family bonding time on this night, and he appreciated the life lessons that his parents and ancestors passed on through those stories more now than ever. An informal family gathering like that was not only a time for its members to be with each other but also a moment for the younger generation to absorb the wisdom of the past. This night, he gazed at the starry night sky on his own and faced many dangers and challenges by himself. As he reminisced about his past star gazing experience with his family, he slowly dozed off.

He woke up hearing the loud beating of waves against the sides of the boat. The rain was coming down hard and heavy. The quiet, starry night quickly turned into a stormy one in less than an hour. That was how fast the weather conditions could change at sea. It certainly caught everyone by surprise. However, everyone was glad to get some rain water to quench their thirst and cool them off. That night, it rained nonstop and slowly filled up the boat with water. Viet looked through some openings in the tarp and could see some monster waves as high as a 30-story building. The wind gusts were loud, and they tossed powerful waves against the rickety, little boat. Viet never encountered such high waves and strong wind gusts like that before except in movies. Those high waves dumped much more water into the boat, which was already full of rainwater. The boat was tossed from one side to the other like a balloon on a windy day. The loud thunder and bright lightning added greater effects to this whole scary show to everyone in the boat. Without encouragement, everyone began praying loudly and vigorously. Everyone thought they might die that night. The boat would either capsize due to powerful waves and strong wind gusts or sink to the bottom of the ocean because it took on so much water from the rain and the relentless waves.

Everyone was wet, cold, exhausted, and scared. But, none wanted to stop praying. The Buddhists were saying their own prayers, while the Catholics started out with the Lord's Prayer. Then, they realized that they might not have enough time for that long prayer before the violent waves engulfed the whole boat. They quickly switched to a shorter prayer and settled with the Hail Mary Prayer with the hope that God would get their SOS message faster and come to their aid immediately. Amidst the turmoil and threat of impending death, the entire boat was filled with prayers. They all joined their voices in prayer and invoked divine power to save them from the violent storm.

Before long, the Buddhists were praying the Hail Mary and the Catholics were reciting the Buddhist prayer. Even though it was a long night and the boat took in lots of water, they thankfully survived that violent storm and their lives were miraculously spared. For Viet, this was certainly another miracle that he experienced on his way to the Promised Land.

Viet's scary encounter with a huge storm reminded him of a couple stories in the Bible. The first was about Jonah as he tried to run away from the Lord's mission for him to the city of Nineveh by calling it to repent. He jumped in a ship and decided to skip town. What he did not know was that he could run from the Lord, but could not hide from Him. The Lord caught up with him by sending a huge storm that frightened all his boat mates. They finally decided that Jonah was bad luck, and they threw him out of the boat to appease an angry God. As Jonah was sinking to the bottom of the sea, the Lord sent a huge whale to take him into its belly and save him. It was a miracle that Jonah was saved, and the Lord kept him safe from that dangerous storm. The other story that involved a scary storm was when the disciples were in the boat with Jesus at night. They found themselves in the middle of the sea and ran into a huge storm. The waves were so powerful that the disciples thought that their boat might sink. They woke Jesus from his sleep and asked him to calm the waves and silence the storm. He let them experience a great miracle and saved their lives that night.

A new day came with a beautiful dawn, and the sea was totally calm as if nothing happened the night before. The captain gave a quick report on the boat's condition after the violent storm and trying to pump water out of the boat. Thankfully, no fatalities were sustained, but the boat did suffer a major damage at the bow—the waves caused a big crack. That meant the captain had to be extra careful with the boat, but he was not sure how long it would hold together on the rough sea. He also shared that the storm threw the boat off course, and they were floating into an unknown territory. Viet went up on the deck to get some fresh air and could not believe what he saw around the boat. There were several sharks lurking around it. He learned in school that the South Pacific is the home for Tiger sharks and a few other species. He also heard that some fishermen in Saigon had caught sharks with human limbs in their stomachs. Now, he had come close to sharks and saw them with his own eyes. If the boat capsized or had broken up in the storm over night, the sharks would have been right there to tear them apart and consume them. Even now, the boat could still break apart, and they all could easily be the victims of a shark attack.

Unfortunately, the sharks were the least of their problems. What Viet did not realize was the impending, deadly danger that he and his boat mates would have to face soon—pirates. Like many young boys, Viet loved pirate stories in his childhood, along with their sense of mystery and adventure. These stories took him to a strange land and let him explore a life of freedom and adventure. They were also fun-filled and intriguing. But, pirates are real and their actions carry deadly consequences. They rob people at gun point in the vast ocean and sometimes hurt or kill their victims. Viet would soon have to face pirates personally and suffer horrible consequences. The captain once again reminded the entire boat that the biggest threat was not the vast ocean, a huge storm, the wild sharks, or the Communist ships. Rather, it was the deadly pirates. Everyone had heard horrible stories about how they robbed refugees at sea, raped the women, killed the men, kidnapped people, and caused all sorts of heartache for many families. The main goal for the captain and the entire group for the remainder of the trip was to elude pirates while searching for a rescue ship. What they did not know was that they would become victims of piracy during this harrowing trip.

Suddenly, the captain dropped his binoculars and pointed to a little black dot at the end of the horizon and said, "Pirates! Pirates!" He then ordered the boat to turn in a certain direction away from the pirate boat, while others ensured he had not misidentify it. Viet had access to a pair of binoculars and could not believe his eyes. He saw a black flag with a skull and two crossed bones flying at the top of the boat mast. Immediately, he felt like he just swallowed a big elephant down his throat.

The boat zig zagged from one end of the horizon to another to avoid the first pirate boat. They thought that was the end of the whole piracy problem. Next, however, they had to dodge another ship, then another one, and even a few more. Before long, their count of the pirate boats was more than a dozen. They also kept their distance from the ships of other Communist countries to avoid any trouble.

They felt that the pirates were closing in on them, and they had nowhere to run. Suddenly, a pirate boat appeared less than fifty yards away, and they saw their nightmare slowly coming true. They first saw the pirate flag of a skull and two crossed bones and some rough-looking folks on the boat deck. As that pirate boat drew closer, they saw at least a dozen men armed with guns, machetes, and other weapons. They pulled their boat right next to ours and began to ask us what we were doing. There was a breakdown of communication. Viet's boat mates and the captain had a tough time understanding the pirates and vice versa. Next thing they knew, the pirates jumped onto the boat and took control. They began to separate men and women to opposite ends of the boat search for jewelry and other valuables. After robbing everyone, they sexually assaulted and raped the women and beat up the men. The whole horrible ordeal went on for about an hour, but it seemed like forever.

Clearly, all the early talk of putting up some resistance and protecting the women went right out of the window. The men could do nothing to fight the evil power, to push back the injustice, or to stand up for the weak and the vulnerable. Like the rest of his boat mates, Viet took the beating and felt helpless with tears rolling down his face. He felt angry with the pirates and their violent, criminal acts against the helpless. This terrible experience left a deep scar on Viet's conscience and moved him to identify himself with the victims of various tragedies and deliver swift justice to all predators. He would have a tough time in the future forgiving the guilty and objecting to the idea of capital punishment. However, he was not the only one who would hold a long-time resentment toward his neighboring countries. Some of their citizens had no conscience and exploited the plight of refugees, particularly the Vietnamese, instead of helping them. If it was up to Viet, he would hang all these low-life, scumbags and other criminals without any regret. Most of his countrymen, especially the refugees, agreed with his thinking regarding justice to some horrible members of their neighboring countries.

These feelings of hatred and not forgiving unfortunately went contrary to Viet's Christian teachings. His Lord Jesus once said, "You have heard that it was said, 'Love your neighbor and hate your enemies.' But I tell you: Love your enemies and pray for those who persecute you, that you may be sons and daughters of your Father in Heaven. He causes His sun to rise on the evil and the good, and sends rain on the righteous and the unrighteous. If you love those who love you, what reward will you get? Are not even the tax collectors doing that? And if you greet only your brothers and sisters, what are you doing more than others? Do not even pagans do that? Be perfect, therefore, as your heavenly Father is perfect (Matthew 5:43-48)." Certainly, Viet did not want to go contrary to this teaching and his Lord's desire for His disciples. Over the years, Viet has softened up and learned to accept "the life sentence" idea and slowly let go of the "death sentence" judgment for horrible crimes. It has certainly been a long process of conversion for Viet, and he still struggles to show mercy and forgiveness to cold-blooded criminals over their heinous crimes.

Viet and his boat mates were badly shaken over the nightmarish incident with the pirates, but thankful that they were all still alive. They pulled themselves together, wiped off each other's tears and blood, started the boat engine, and headed out to the unknown again. Most of them did not know one another before this trip, and they all had different backgrounds and religions. As the search for freedom brought them together on this dangerous, uncertain trip, now their resolve to stay alive and make it to the Promised Land or a refugee camp pushed them forward. What they did not know was that this last encounter with the pirates was just the beginning of a long series of pirate encounters that were yet to come.

The boat headed away from the horrible spot and actively searched for friendly ships that could rescue them while trying to avoid pirate boats. But, pirates were like a pack of piranhas that patrolled certain parts of the ocean looking for victims. After riding and scanning the ocean for a couple of hours, they spotted a dozen ships that they assumed would be friendly. They began to talk among themselves to determine who could speak a foreign language to communicate with the occupants of those ships. The two most common languages that might be helpful in communicating with rescuers would be English and French. While cruising along in search for friendly ships, another pirate boat came out of nowhere to confront them.

Everyone on the boat was caught completely by surprise and quickly had a weary look on their tired faces. The sense of peace that they felt a moment ago seemed to vanish in a blink of an eye. Without saying a word, all their eyes wanted to scream out, "Oh no! Not again!" But, before they could come up with a good defensive plan, a group of strangers took control of the boat and began to do almost the same things as did the last group of pirates. They separated men and women and took whatever valuables that were left. After committing violent and barbaric acts, they left everyone a little more shook up and devastated compared to the last time.

If these thoughtless pirates assumed that they might have intimidated or defeated the group, they were wrong. What they did drew the group closer to one another and motivated them to search for their freedom and keep surviving this sort of ordeal. Again, they were thankful to be alive. They chalked up their losses and thought that things could be worse. They could have killed everyone and thrown everyone overboard or set the whole boat on fire. Indeed, no one would have ever known. That is the law of the jungle, and Viet and his boat mates learned to survive it. Out in the wide-open ocean, whoever has a bigger gun can make others do whatever he or she wants.

Once again, the boat people dusted off the horrible experience and continued their quest for freedom and a new life. They kept their heads high, bound each other's wounds, and lifted each other up with words of encouragement. But, what they did not know was they would run into yet other pirate boats several more times. They were robbed and cleaned out right down to their undergarments. These pirates even took everyone's clothing and most of the boat's fuel. They did not have much fuel left and that caused everyone to be concerned that they might be stranded at sea indefinitely. Adding to the problem of fuel shortage, the boat took a big hit by the monster waves on that stormy night. There was a big crack on its bow, and it was slowly taking in quite a bit of water. No one knew how long the boat could withstand the relentless ocean waves and continue to stay afloat.

Still, the group plowed ahead and kept searching for friendly ships that would rescue them, all the while praying for divine help and protection. Unfortunately, as soon as they again spotted a ship on the horizon and headed toward it, it would quickly disappear. The horrible encounters with a handful of pirate boats had caused them to take extreme precautions and be careful about approaching other ships and boats.

Viet and his boat mates might have felt that they had extreme experiences with their encounters with the pirate boats. Only later did they learn that other refugees had run-ins with pirates more than a dozen of times. Some refugees were killed or disappeared without a trace. It is certainly harrowing to be a refugee. One must leave his or her home with few belongings except one's clothes and a few miscellaneous items and head into the unknown—one that is full of danger and harm.

Viet and his boat mates thought they were done with pirates and life troubles. What they did not realize was a new, impending problem facing them. The last group of scumbag pirates took everything including the group's food and water. They would soon face hunger and thirst without any possibility of being rescued. Viet had never faced this dilemma, even when he was in the Communist prison for trying to sneak out of the country. The food in prison was revolting, but at least he did not starve to death.

Viet did not know what he and his boat mates would do with nothing to eat or drink in the days ahead. Would they all die? Would the whole trip simply be a journey of death and a complete failure?

The whole idea of death never entered Viet's mind, but it seemed more real now than ever. He began to pray harder and tried to bargain with God. Like Abraham who bargained with God on the number of righteous people living in Sodom to save this sinful city from God's wrath, Viet wanted to make a deal with God to save his life. Apparently, Abraham asked God to spare Sodom and not obliterate it if he could find 50 righteous people in that sinful city. Unfortunately, he could not find that many good folks and had to settle for ten in the end. Similarly, Viet called on his Lord to save his life. In turn, Viet promised to dedicate his life to serving God and His Church.

While Viet was busy praying and making deals with God, his boat captain started to talk about the idea of cannibalism to help the boat's occupants prepare for difficult days ahead. This subject came up because the pirates took all the food and drink supplies and anything they considered valuable. To the entire boat, the captain said, "We have been through a lot the last 24 hours. We had to face one pirate boat after another, so far almost a dozen of them. Thankfully, none of us was killed or thrown overboard. However, we have a problem. Those bastard pirates took everything from us, even our food and water. I'm afraid we won't have anything more to eat, and we might die of starvation. So, I want to prepare you all for that harsh reality and unpleasant ending."

As the boat captain paused and glanced around the entire boat, everyone had a sad and despondent look on their face. Then, the whole boat became quiet. The only sounds they heard were the waves crashing against the boat. Awkwardly, the boat captain continued, "I hate to say this, but we might have to eat each other to stay alive. What I mean is this: In case one of us dies, can you eat a boat mate because of our lack of food? Just think about that!"

Viet had never given the idea of cannibalism any thought until that moment. However, he had read about it in various novels and recently watched a movie that discussed it in a tragic story of a sports team. Apparently, a rugby team flew to a country in South America for a game. Unfortunately, the team's plane had a mechanical problem and crashed into the Andes Mountains. No one came to their rescue quickly, and the survivors had to hunker down and survive on their own for more than three weeks in the cold, snowy environment. Soon, they ran out of food and resorted to cannibalism to survive. Surely, that experience forever changed the group of survivors. Yet, anyone who dared to go through such an experience and did the unthinkable by eating one's own kind survived the ordeal.

Viet could not imagine himself going through with it. The whole idea of cannibalism gave him a chill down his spine. He felt nauseous and overwhelmed just thinking about what he might do survive. He realized, however, that if he did not go through with the idea, he would quickly die of starvation. After some prayers and tough consideration, he accepted the idea of cannibalism and consuming his deceased boat mates to stay alive. By accepting the idea, he also had to agree to let his boat mates eat him if he died before they did.

The boat's occupants engaged in an emotional and painful discussion about the idea of cannibalism. Tears and anguish were plentiful. Many of the women did not want to go through with it, whereas most of the men reluctantly accepted it. No doubt, this was a harrowing time and one of the most difficult moments in the entire trip. They truly might face a life-and-death decision and would have to decide to go one way or the other. What Viet did not know was that this tough, hypothetical decision sharpened his mind and helped prepare him for many important decisions yet to come in his life. Although the decision to potentially participate in cannibalism was tough, trying to figure out what they might have to do with the pirates was not easy either. They could all be dead if they decided to resist and fight. Sadly, they chose to take the beatings, be robbed, and be raped; indeed, that was the best option for staying alive.

Until that moment, Viet had not imagined the valuable lessons that real life could teach him. He had learned a lot in school and classrooms and did quite well in academic and theoretical environments. But, out here in real life, he certainly gained many valuable life lessons and absorbed practical knowledge that would help him in the future. These lessons prepared him for future challenges and would carry him throughout his lifetime. Among the lessons that Viet took away from this harrowing trip included making tough decisions that most people would never ever have to even consider in their lifetime. This ability would help Viet face his future challenges without much fear and see his options clearly in times of discernment. For Viet, his decision to accept and potentially go through with the whole idea of cannibalism would forever change him, whether he had to do it or not. Most of his boat mates made the same decision, whereas only some could not muster up enough nerve and courage to face it.

With his Christian faith, Viet learned that one of the sacraments—the Holy Eucharist—addresses the idea of eating the body of his Lord Jesus and drinking His blood. Many of Viet's Christian friends believe in that idea and consume the Holy Eucharist as the real body and blood of their Lord. Some Christians, unfortunately, do not believe in the real presence of Jesus in the Holy Eucharist. They think the bread and wine simply symbolize the body and blood of Jesus. They cannot comprehend the whole idea of the real body and blood of their Lord in the Eucharist. To do so would mean they must accept and endorse the idea of cannibalism in the Sacrament of the Holy Eucharist. In general, the public and some Christians do not like the idea.

Everyone seems to cringe at the thought of eating the flesh, sinus, or bones of another human being. Everyone also realizes that a human being will die without food and nourishment or eating and drinking. Jesus certainly encouraged His disciples and followers to eat His flesh and drink His blood if they wanted eternal life. Like the rest of the public, Viet did not appreciate his life or the gift of life until he was at the brink of losing it. But, the only way for him to stay alive was to eat and drink whatever was available. It was simply a matter of survival, and he might have to do the impossible, including practicing cannibalism.

If Viet or his boat mates wanted to stay alive, they would need to find nourishment any way possible, including cannibalizing another human. Similarly, a Christian must do the impossible and consume the body and blood of his or her Lord Jesus to stay alive. But, unlike the flesh and blood of a human being or any earthly nourishment, the body and blood of Jesus is the divine source of nourishment; hence, it has divine power. Viet could see why consuming the body and blood of his Lord would bring him divine strength and help and ultimately eternal life.

As Viet began to accept the idea of cannibalism, the boat captain loudly announced, "Look over there! A big ship that could save us!" Everyone suddenly forgot about the horrible and morbid conversation about cannibalism. They rushed to catch up with the ship and prayed that it would be the ship of their salvation. Their boat worked hard to move toward the ship as fast as it could while the captain carefully double-checked to ensure it was a friendly ship. Unlike other ships, this one did not run away or show any hostile signs. In fact, it seemed to be moving toward Viet's boat and letting them know that it saw them.

They did not know to which country this ship belonged. Then, the boat captain shouted in a joyous voice, "It is circling us! That is a good sign! That is the international way of checking out a boat before rescuing it!" After a long week at sea facing turmoil and near-death experiences, Viet and his boat mates finally saw signs of hope and salvation. They felt like they were about to receive help and guidance on their way to the Promised Land or the Gate of Heaven.

Chapter 8

The Miraculous Rescue

It was one of the most beautiful sights that Viet and his boat mates had seen for nearly a week as they all climbed up from the bottom of the boat. Like Jesus coming out of the tomb after the third day or a dead person rising from the dead, everyone looked toward the right side of the boat toward the big ship.

The boat captain said, "See that big ship over there!"

Everyone responded, "Wow! Look how big it is!"

They were still at least several hundred meters from the ship. This was the sight about which they had been dreaming and for which they had been waiting for days after the terrible ordeals they had endured at sea. They faced deadly storms and other dangers of the sea such as sharks, the hot sun, sea sickness, and potential drowning. They worried about being caught and put in prison by Communists, including the Vietnamese authorities. They suffered physical, verbal, and mental abuse from pirates, along with beatings, rapes, and robbing. They endured hunger and thirst; both cold and hot temperatures; loneliness, hopelessness, and fear; and other harmful threats including being continually wet from the ocean and rain. They endured these trials in search of freedom and a new life. Worst of all, they confronted their mortality, or death, and the horrible idea of cannibalism—all on their way to the Promised Land.

Like many of his boat mates, Viet was completely oblivious about death and not fearful of it at all. His ability to not fear death became a great asset for him later in life. If Viet was not even afraid of death, then nothing in this life could scare him. Perhaps his fearless attitude could help him overcome many life challenges and make it to the Promised Land at all cost. By facing all the ordeals on this harrowing journey, Viet could now appreciate the long, tough journey that God's people underwent to make it to the Promised Land. He also experienced the exhilarating feeling that God's people had upon seeing the Promised Land as he looked at the ship that was set to save him.

Unlike many ships of which the group had caught a glimpse from afar during this journey, this ship did not try to run away from them or show any hostile signs. Viet and his companions began to feel hopeful and confident that this ship would rescue them from their current situation and take them to the Promised Land. Perhaps prayers do work, and God finally answered Viet's prayers after a week of patiently waiting and enduring trials! Just then, the voice of the boat's captain emerged to confirm Viet's upbeat feeling. He said, "This ship is coming toward us!"

Viet assumed that was a good thing, but still none of his boat mates had positively identified the ship as friend or foe. All they could hope for now was that it was a friendly one. Next, they could see the ship begin to circle the tiny, rickety boat. Trailing waves formed quickly behind the ship, and they tossed the little boat right to left. They were all afraid that the boat might capsize on the brink of their salvation and all would drown. That would be horrible!

As they hung on to the boat, the captain tried to reassure them about the ship. "What they are doing right now is absolutely right. They have to circle our boat three times according to international law before they can do anything." Viet had never heard of such a law and did not know his boat captain had such wide knowledge of law and rescue. But, this law seemed to be a bit dangerous, because it appeared to endanger lives and risked killing the smaller boat's occupants. Then, the captain reminded them, "Try not to gather all on one side of the boat, because that could tip over the entire boat, especially under those trailing waves of the ship. Let's distribute the weight of the boat evenly. Some of you need to go to the other side of the boat."

Suddenly, the ship stopped, and everyone breathed the sigh of relief. But, no one knew what was going to happen next. What needed to happen first, however, between the small boat and the big ship was the ability to communicate with each other. The boat mates began to encourage one another to brush up their limited and rusty language abilities. Two languages they decided to use to communicate with the big ship were English and French. It was already difficult to think and put thoughts together in a cohesive manner, let alone in a foreign language. In an exhausted and broken voice, a few yelled out in English: "Save us! SOS!" Several more called out in French, saying, "Salvi!"

The next thing they saw coming down to the upper deck of the gigantic ship was half a dozen people who looked a bit Asian. The whole boat was hoping these people were not from North Korea or China. That would be bad news because they might be allies with the Vietnamese Communists and would take everyone back to prison. Suddenly, these folks responded, "Okay! All right!" Then, they asked, "Where are you going?" A couple of the men on the boat answered in broken English, "Anywhere! Please save!" Next, the crew of the ship disappeared for a while; we presume they were discussing how to deal with these refugees.

The next ten minutes felt like an eternity. At first, Viet thought the men on the ship would simply distribute some food and drink and then abandon them. Their hope of being saved would dash into thin air. The group also realized that if the ship chose to pick the refugees up, and none of the refugee camps wanted to take them in, the ship would be stuck with all the responsibilities of taking care of their rescued souls. All Viet could pray for at this moment was that the men on the ship had caring and compassionate hearts and would choose to pick him up and take the group to a refugee camp. If they were selfish and uncaring, they would simply wash their hands of the group. Viet believed that there were still a lot of good and loving people in the world. After a short period of waiting, the crew showed up again on the ship's deck. They threw down to the small boat a long rope ladder and called for them to climb up on the side of the ship.

Surely, this was the moment of jubilation and salvation for Viet and his boat mates. He and his boat mates had been praying for this moment for more than a week and now they are really experiencing it. They had finally been saved! Even though they might not know what was waiting ahead or where they might be heading, for now they knew they were moving up from the bottom of that rickety boat to a large, safe ship. God had made this happen by sending them a rope ladder from above. That miraculous ladder reminded Viet of Jacob's ladder, which he had read about in the Bible.

The symbol of a ladder is important in the Christian tradition, as well as in the Jewish and Islamic faiths. Even in secular tradition, stories such as "Jack and the Beanstalk" borrowed the idea of a ladder to express the human desire to be free from one's current situation of confinement and misfortune and extend great hope for a better life.

Jacob's ladder embraces the same thoughts and much more. Apparently, Jacob, with the help of his mother, tricked his father Isaac to receive the sacred, ancestral blessing on his future. That cunning act caused his older brother Esau to become furious and hunt him down to kill him. Jacob then went into hiding and became exhausted to the point of passing out beneath a tree. In his sweet dream, he saw a ladder connecting earth to Heaven. That ladder represented God's blessings upon him and his posterity. God promised to be with Jacob and help his posterity to multiply abundantly like sand on the seashores or stars in the sky. One can only imagine how that ladder boosted Jacob's self-confidence and courage to stand up for himself and begin a new life with God. Like Jacob, that rope ladder gave Viet new-found strength and hope to face the challenges ahead and begin a new life away from his homeland.

Along with his boat mates, Viet looked up that long rope ladder and rushed toward it before it was pulled away from him. He never had a treehouse growing up and had no experience climbing this kind of ladder. It swayed back and forth in mid-air as the first few people began to climb it. They hung on for dear life as the wind tossed the ladder back and forth like a dry leaf, as the waves ferociously pounded against the side of the ship beneath the ladder. The waves were doing their best to add a dramatic effect to their struggles to get to the top. A hand slip or even a small distraction would plunge the climber into the ocean to be consumed by the violent, deadly waves. For Viet, faith was like that ladder swinging in the wind. One needs to hang on tight to it in tough times and does not let go. Otherwise, one would find oneself hurt, lost, bitter, disappointed, or overwhelmed by life's challenges. Worse yet, one might be temporarily or permanently separated from one's God and Creator.

Soon it was Viet's turn to climb up that miraculous rope ladder, and he found himself right below it. He turned to the small crowd standing behind him and said, "Let's go, my friends! Let's climb! This is what we've been praying and hoping for." Then, he grabbed the ladder to pull himself up. He put his first foot on it and then his other foot. Next thing he knew, he was climbing. He slowly rose a bit higher and higher. Soon, he was far away from the crowd and that old fishing boat. The eureka moment arrived when he reached the top and stepped onto the deck of the huge ship, reuniting with some of his boat mates who had gone ahead of him.

It was a totally different world where Viet was standing. He looked around, and his view of the earthly world had miraculously transformed into a Heavenly one. The sun was sending its warm, spectacular rays of sunshine throughout God's beautiful creation, while the air seemed to offer not just life but also joy and great promises. His old boat and lots of earthly things looked tiny and insignificant from Viet's vantage point. Perhaps, this is how it would look in Heaven. He felt privileged to have a glimpse of it.

As Viet was soaking in the feelings of jubilation and triumph on the ship's deck, he recalled the Bible story of the Transfiguration and the overwhelming emotions that the three disciples experienced on Mount Tabor. One day, Jesus took three of His favorite disciples—Peter, James, and John—up to the high mountain to reveal Himself and give them an awesome experience of a lifetime. These disciples were shown the glory of God and the joy of Heaven that no human experienced before or has experienced since. They enjoyed and appreciated it so much that they did not want to leave the high mountain and asked Jesus to stay there forever. This was exactly how Viet felt at the moment he stood on top of that huge ship. He felt as if he was on top of the world, and Jesus was right by his side. All the danger and suffering he had endured in that tiny boat and the world below could no longer worry or threaten him. For, in some way, he had made it to the Promised Land and had been miraculously saved by the amazing grace of God. He now could leave everything behind, including the old world, to begin his joyful new life and bright, promising future.

As he looked down on his tiny rickety boat, Viet saw the strong waves slowly push it away further and further from the big ship. Part of him could not wait to watch the big waves swamp it and pull it down to the bottom of the deep ocean along with its memories of suffering, hunger, thirst, piracy, loneliness, hopelessness, starvation, thoughts of cannibalism, and death in the past week. The boat also reminded him of the Viet Nam War, its aftermath, years suffering under the Communist government, and half a dozen failed attempts to escape the country. A few of those times landed him in prison and caused him to endure torture and abuse by the prison guards and other inmates. Despite all those horrible memories, the boat held everyone together during that dark, stormy night and inspired them to help one another and keep their chins up after the barbaric pirate assaults. Another part of Viet felt sad that he was saying goodbye to "an old faithful friend" who had been through tough times with him and kept him alive. He was overwhelmed by emotions, and tears began to roll down his cheeks. He waved to the boat one last time and turned to the boat captain. "What will happen to the boat?" he asked. The captain answered, "Oh, the waves will take it out to the open sea, and eventually it will capsize and sink." Before long, the tiny boat grew smaller and disappeared from their sight.

The entire group gathered at the center of the huge ship for some photos and instructions as its captain began to address them. He welcomed them in broken English, but his English was definitely better than theirs. He told them that his ship was a South Korean tanker on its way to Singapore. "Thank God he said, 'South Korea, instead of North Korea'," Viet thought. Otherwise, they would be in a lot of trouble again and would have to escape the Communists again! The captain then asked, "Do you want me to drop you off in Singapore or somewhere else?" For a refugee, Singapore would be like Heaven on earth. Other possible places were Malaysia, Indonesia, Philippines, or Thailand. But, most refugees preferred Singapore because evidently, they would be treated like kings and queens there. Without hesitation, everyone answered in unison, "Yes! Singapore!" Even though they all wanted to be taken to Singapore, they were not quite sure what life would be like there or whether they would accept the group into its refugee camp.

Before they could even discuss that new land, they were invited to the crews' dining room for some food and drink. The ship's captain and his crew knew the refugees were starved and thirsty after being in the boat for days. The dining room was located on the other end of the ship. As Viet began to walk, he looked and saw big steel boxes stacked up neatly row after row in the middle of the ship's deck. The boxes were commercial containers with a big U.S.A label on each of them. He realized the ship was actually a business tanker from South Korea. Its captain and crew were kind and compassionate enough to rescue Viet and his boat mates from their miserable situation.

Viet could not believe there were still good people like the captain and the crew of his tanker in the world. This day was not just the day of salvation for him. It was also the day that his faith in humanity was restored. All the doubt and suspicion that the Communists caused between him and his countrymen suddenly disappeared.

The ship's captain and its crew were complete strangers, but they saw a stranded boat in the middle of the ocean carrying human beings that had been robbed, raped, beaten, and left for dead by pirates. They were moved to reach out and save their fellow human beings. They did not have to do what they did and could have treated them like other ships, ignoring them and sailing away. But, their hearts were moved with pity, and they stopped to pick up the refugees. They hoisted everyone up onto their ship, washed them up, gave them clothing to wear and food to eat. Then, they took Viet and his boat mates to the best refugee camp, which happened to be in Singapore. They were not afraid to take care of the paperwork and other costs to help these misfortunate refugees. Viet was deeply moved by the human care and compassion of these strangers. They had become his neighbors and came to his aid in his time of need.

Viet was reminded of a similar story that he read in the Gospels. It was the story of the Good Samaritan (Luke 10:29-37). A Jewish man was travelling from Jerusalem to Jericho and fell victim to thieves. They robbed him, beat him up, and left him half dead on the side of the road. A priest passed by the same road and saw the poor victim, but decided to cross on the other side. Later that day, a Levite walked down the same road and did the same thing. Then, a Samaritan happened to go down that exact road and witnessed the horrible scene by the roadside. He saw the poor man who was bruised, bleeding, and left for dead. This caring traveler immediately jumped into the ditch, bound up the victim's wounds, hoisted him onto his beast, and took him to the nearby inn. He pulled out several coins to give to the innkeeper and said, "Take good care of him. If you spend more than this, I'll repay you on the way back."

Viet often wondered if kind and generous folks like that Good Samaritan only existed in stories. Growing up in a tough environment with the Communists, he thought everyone was out simply for themselves. He assumed that it was a dog-eat-dog world, and people would not hesitate to take advantage of their neighbors to save themselves. He became callous to the idea of kindness and compassion. Now, however, Viet saw for himself that there were still many people like the Good Samaritan in the world. On this unforgettable day, he met some of them on this gigantic ship and thanked God for the blessing of them in the world. He also realized that God truly sends certain people at the right moment into our lives. They were like God's messengers who come to give Viet and his countrymen a hand and lift their spirits in a tough, hopeless moment. Their lives would not be the same without these kind sailors. They are a sign of God's presence for anyone who dared to believe in the Higher Power and needed help from above.

While Viet was filled with thoughts of appreciation, he was summoned to receive some food, drink, and clothing. He was handed a cold, fresh glass of water after going for days with only a few sips of dirty water. He was reminded to drink it slowly and not try to gulp it quickly, because he might choke on it. Viet remembered taking the first sip of that water and how refreshing it tasted as the clear liquid touched his lips. He thought he was drinking some Heavenly liquid when the cold water flowed down his throat and rejuvenated his whole body. He could feel how sweet and delightful this glass of water tasted in his dry mouth after many days of having little to drink. The cold taste reminded him of the cold drink he used to have on a hot day in his tropical homeland. The sweet taste represented the freedom and blessings of the new life the Lord would give him in a new land. Until he died, he would never forget that out-of-the-body experience after he tasted that amazing cold, fresh glass of water.

Again, Viet could not help but recall a similar experience that a Bible story tells about the guests at a wedding with Jesus (John 2:1-11). Many guests at this wedding celebration apparently drank some water that tasted like the best wine in town. This miraculous story happened at a wedding in Cana. Jesus was invited to that wedding and His mother informed Him that the wedding party ran out of wine. After some initial hesitation, Jesus helped the situation by turning water in six stone water jars (used for Jewish ceremonial washing) into the best wine of all. The headwaiter tasted the water that had become wine and called the bridegroom to say, "Everyone serves good wine first, and then when people have drunk freely, an inferior one; but you have kept the good wine until now" (John 2:10). That was exactly the reaction that Viet had after tasting that cold, fresh water even though it did not turn into wine. The taste was so amazing and out-of-this-world that it was almost like the miraculous taste at the wedding in Cana. This splendid experience of a refreshing taste was something Viet would never forget. Perhaps that is how a spiritually thirsty person feels having God quench his or her thirst with His eternal spring of water.

After finishing that tasty, refreshing glass of water, Viet was given new clothes and shoes and shown to the bathroom for a cleansing shower. It had been more than a week, but Viet and his boat mates had not had any way to clean themselves up. He looked forward to taking a shower and getting his whole body freshened up. Growing up in a tropical place like Viet Nam, Viet sometimes took a shower several times a day. He often went swimming with friends at neighborhood swimming pools or took his shampoo to a fun soccer game in the rain and enjoyed a long shower in the street with friends. He cherished those great memories, but this time there was no playing or having fun in taking a shower. He had to do it out of necessity. Before he stepped into the shower stall, he spotted the toilet and the sink nearby—something different than what he knew back home. His home country was a former French colony; as such, many things had been greatly influenced by the French culture and tradition. For example, the water tank for flushing the toilet was high up and close to the ceiling. Or, the toilet might be flush with the floor level, and one had to squat while using the toilet rather than sitting on it.

But, those were not the only things that were different from what Viet knew as he grew up. The shower and sink back home had only one faucet, and it was for cold water. There was no hot water faucet, because it was a hot, tropical country. If the need arose for hot water to wash one's body, such as when one was sick, one had to boil water for that purpose. Now he stood before two faucets: one with the red letter **H** on the left and the other with the blue letter **C** on the right. Not knowing English that well, Viet did not know what the letters meant. The whole thing was a bit overwhelming as Viet stared at the entire setup not knowing what to do. But, he was afraid to ask because of his limited English ability. Finally, he turned on the left faucet marked **H**, and a powerful stream of hot water burst out. He quickly jumped away before getting burned. Then, he ran back to turn it off. Next, he turned on the right faucet and the opposite happened. A powerful stream of cold water rushed out and again Viet had to switch it off.

He paused and wondered why they even need hot water. He had never used it back home except for cooking. Everyone took a cold shower every day and enjoyed it because it was so hot and muggy all the time. However, the cold water here on the ship was much colder than in Viet Nam. After some quick thinking, Viet turned on both faucets in the shower at the same time. With some minor adjustments, he had the water temperature settled in to a comfortable level. This was the first refreshing shower he had enjoyed for more than a week.

That day, Viet learned his first lesson on Western lifestyle and how to make quick adjustments with a new culture. He also realized that there would be much learning and tough days ahead on his journey to a new life of freedom and great promises. But, he trusted that God and his ancestors would watch over him and guide him. His first shower as a free person on the ship not only taught him how to work the shower itself but also introduced him to the wonderful fragrance of Western soap and shampoo. He felt quite refreshed and smelled fabulous after that first shower beyond the Communists' control. Perhaps, the refreshing water was the taste of freedom and the shower was the smell of success! No longer would he have to get stuck in the oppressing, smelly yoke of Communism. From now on, he could dream big and smell like a million bucks as he moved closer to the Promised Land.

After that refreshing and aromatic shower, Viet was treated to a fantastic lunch. He was served a delicious bowl of noodles, a can of tropical fruit juice, and some cookies for dessert. What made him and his boat mates feel at home with the crew was their use of chopsticks for the meal. Those chopsticks brought them back to the way they used to eat their daily meals at home. The tropical fruit juice also added some familiarity for these refugees and helped them not miss their home country too terribly. But, two other features of this meal made Viet pause a bit and wonder what roles they would play in his new life. Unlike the fresh fruit he had at home for each meal, his juicy drink here in the new world came from a can. He recalled lots of things during the Viet Nam War also came from cans. Another strange thing he encountered at this meal was cookies for dessert. Back home he often had fruit for dessert. Then again, most of his countrymen would forego dessert and drink tea at the end of a meal. Moreover, a typical lunch in Asia would be the biggest meal of the day and certainly bigger than a dinner. That way a person would have enough energy to do his or her work during the day and sleep better after a small dinner. Viet was very thankful for this meal, but intrigued by the features new to him. This was the first peaceful, delicious, cooked meal he had eaten since the night he left his family.

Everyone soon completed lunch and was told to take a quick nap. This custom is part of many Asian countries due to European influences during colonial times. Viet Nam took on a lot more from French culture and language than from American, because it was a French colony for more than two centuries. French Catholic missionaries created its language after studying the original Vietnamese language, which had its roots in Chinese, and combined it with French to create the current Vietnamese. The siesta or nap custom has always been a challenge for young children. Instead, they like to do things all the time and find napping as something that babies and old folks need to do. If someone found him- or herself in downtown Saigon during nap time—from one to three in the afternoon—the whole busy city would be completely deserted, much like a ghost town.

One of the favorite activities for Viet and many of his friends during this time was going swimming at a public pool in the neighborhood. He enjoyed this time with friends back home, but now found himself with strangers on a tanker and not able to talk to anyone beyond a simple greeting due to the language barrier. They spoke mainly Korean and he spoke Vietnamese. Neither side spoke English that well. Viet quickly thought about what he should do during his nap time and decided to take a walk and explore the entire ship a little more.

The huge ship was like a small city. He knew there were many rooms in the control tower, because he was given a quick tour by one of the crew members when he first arrived. Viet was afraid to get lost in the maze, but he pressed onward with his little adventure. He walked out of his room into a small hallway that zigzagged to other rooms such as the dining room, the entertainment room, the exercise room, the game room, the library, the kitchen, and so on. He went down to the lower deck and ended up in several engine and storage rooms. It took forever to get out of that deck, but he finally ended up on the top deck. He was invited into the observation room, which was part of the control tower and the place where the captain and some of his crew ran this tanker. There were lots of windows, meter dials, knobs, and buttons, including a giant steering wheel. After visiting for several minutes, Viet said goodbye to the captain and his crew and left this special room. He decided to go down to the main deck to check out the steel boxes he had seen earlier. There were at least a dozen rows of them stacked up neatly about five-boxes high. These boxes took up almost the whole deck and created a huge skyscraper-like block. It took Viet quite some time to walk around it. As he looked out into the vast ocean from his high vantage point on the ship's deck, he saw a calm, beautiful, blue ocean that seemed to stretch out beyond the horizon. Viet had heard the phrase "deep, blue ocean," but this was the first time he saw it with his own eyes. The blue water was mesmerizing and had a calming effect on its onlookers. But, Viet also realized that just a day ago this calm blue ocean had tried to swallow him whole with a violent storm. Viet spent some time on the open deck to soak in the cool breeze and the magnificent view of the ocean while thinking of his family and friends that he left behind. He also thought of the uncertain future waiting ahead of him.

As he was deep in his thoughts, a crew member called out to him, "Heh! Come in. It's time for dinner." Viet did not realize it was already early evening, and everyone would eat dinner a bit sooner than his usual time at home, which was around 6:30 or 7 pm. Although this was his first dinner on the ship, it was an amazing one. Perhaps it was not like a fancy meal on a cruise ship, but at least he did not have to eat a cold-cut meal with pirates. He, along with his boat mates and the entire crew of the ship, was served a huge piece of steak with rice and small pieces of potatoes. Those pieces of potatoes were called "French fries." Viet did not know why they were called that. Maybe the French invented those fries and cooked them that way. Meanwhile, the crew introduced Viet and his boat mates to ketchup and told them to eat it with their French fries. The whole thing tasted kind of funny—a bit sweet and oily. The rice also looked and tasted a funny. It was not completely white like the kind of rice he remembered at home and was called "Uncle Ben's" according to the crew. The steak looked somewhat oily and a bit red.

Most of the food in a third-world country need to be well-cooked to avoid food poisoning and bacteria-related illnesses. Viet's piece of steak looked like it was undercooked and still bleeding. But, Viet was taught to be grateful and not demanding, especially after everything the crew had done for him and his boat mates on this vast ocean. Besides, it was a bit too much meat for one person to consume. At home, the piece of steak on his plate alone would be served an entire family. He felt guilty eating that much meat by himself. He was also confused about what to do with that big piece of steak. Most of the meat, fish, and vegetables at home were cut into small pieces before cooking. While he was still bewildered, a crew member approached him and showed him how to cut up the steak along its grain with the steak knife while holding it down with the fork. Then, he passed him a bottle of A-1 steak sauce to be used with his bleeding, reddish steak. This was the first time Viet had ever used a fork and a steak knife to cut a piece of meat at a dining table. He was told to hold the fork in one hand and the steak knife on the other to eat this dinner. After some awkward moments, Viet enjoyed his first Western dinner on this cruise-ship-like tanker. Adding to that classic meal, he was given his first can of Coca-Cola. He had seen its picture in various literature after the Viet Nam War, but that was the first time he took his first sip of this classic American drink.

Directly after the group finished dinner, everyone was invited to the entertainment room and treated to a movie titled, *Twenty Thousand League under the Sea*. Most of them could not understand English well enough to appreciate this classic movie, but they were able to follow along a little bit. What Viet found ironic was that they were watching an ocean adventure while being in the middle of the ocean themselves. The movie lasted a couple of hours, and then the ship's captain sent everyone to bed. He also let them know that the ship would arrive in Singapore the next morning.

That night, Viet became a bit restless even though he was tired. As he tossed and turned thinking about his uncertain future and what was waiting ahead for him, he recalled the scripture story about Joseph, who was sold by his brothers to Egyptian merchants and was transported to a foreign land. Joseph must have been restless, worried, and a bit scared during that journey. But, he totally put his trust in the Lord who had a plan for his life, his family, and the world around him. Only much later and after much personal suffering did Joseph realize what the Lord intended his life to be and why he had to zigzag through that tough, winding journey. Similarly, Viet shared the feelings that Joseph had to go through on his way to the foreign land. As soon as Viet realized this and put his faith in the Lord, he peacefully closed his eyes for the night and slept.

Before long, the sun rose and a beautiful new day welcomed Viet and his boat mates. The ship continued toward its destination, and later that morning it docked on one of the sea ports in Singapore. The refugees all said, "Thank you" to the captain and his crew and had a tearful farewell with them as they were given addresses to be pen pals. Viet made friends with the ship's captain and obtained his home address in South Korea. They both promised each other to keep in touch. This was another time that Viet realized God sends certain good folks throughout one's life and allows lives cross for a great purpose. It was no accident that the ship's captain and his crew came to Viet's rescue and brought him to safety. Among the bad, evil, and cunning folks of the world, there are still a lot of good, caring, and kind people who open their hearts and homes to help others without worrying about the costs. This crew risked their lives, reputation, and resources to help Viet and his countrymen. If Singapore did not agree to take them in, the ship's captain and crew would be responsible for them and would have to take care of them. But, for one reason or another, they allowed the love of God and their care for other human beings drive them to reach out to Viet's boat in their time of need. They also took them to a safe resting area as they waited and tried to find their way to the Promised Land. They certainly continued the work of God's salvation that God's Son Jesus started more than two thousand years ago on the Cross. They helped make Viet's world a little brighter and keep evil, dark power at bay. Viet's trust and hope in humanity was renewed and strengthened after his encounter with this South Korean tanker and its crew.

Chapter 9

Camp Freedom in a Foreign Land

The tanker finally pulled into a sea port and arrived at a dock in Singapore where they saw boats and ships of all sizes. They also saw a couple of empty buses parked on the dock. There was no banner, fanfare, or big crowd waiting to cheer and welcome them. That is indeed the life of a refugee. Viet and his boat mates officially became refugees. But, at least on the way down from the big ship, this time they did not have to use the rope ladder as they did on the way up. Instead, they walked down to the dock on a nice, sturdy stairway. Once they were on the ground, they all turned around and waved to the crew one last time, thanking them for saving and showing these refugees great hospitality on the ship. They also thanked God for letting them land safely on this foreign land and stay alive despite havoc and danger along the way. That must be how the people of God must have felt when they crossed the Red Sea and landed safely on dry land. They were grateful to the loving God who did everything to save them. Viet personally knelt on the ground and kissed it to show a sign of respect and appreciation for the country that granted him and his boat mates a temporary refugee while they tried to find a permanent home in another country.

Viet and the others boarded the two buses and were taken to a camp, which was located away from a big city or civilization. They finally arrived at the camp and approached its front gates. The camp was surrounded by high walls of barbed wire and secured with big gates and well-armed guards. Someone on their bus said out loud, "It looks like a prison!" Another countered, "I'd rather be in this prison than the one at home with the Communists!" After some exchanges between the bus driver and the guards, the gates opened and the buses entered. Viet looked back on the gates and wondered when he would ever be able to get out of this camp.

Everyone was taken to the biggest house in the middle of the camp for paperwork and initial interviews. This process lasted for several hours. Next, the group was divided and sent to various houses in the camp. Viet was under eighteen and had no family members. He was sent to the "orphanage" house. No one was there to greet or welcome him except a camp official who had walked with him after finishing the paperwork at the big house. With nothing much in his hands, he was led to a bunkbed in the corner of the room and told to take the bottom one. At least a dozen bunkbeds were in that room. Viet sat down on the bed for a little bit to catch his breath and soak in everything that had just happened. He could not believe that after many failed attempts to sneak out of Viet Nam, he finally made it to a refugee camp. He felt a sense of completion and satisfaction. Now, however, he wondered what would happen to him and how his future might turn out. He felt like fish out of water and worried about what tomorrow might bring.

While Viet was wondering about his future beyond the camp, the head of the house who was also the director of the camp walked toward him and introduced himself. His name was Mr. Sinh. He tried to explain a whole bunch of things in English, but everything just went right over Viet's head due to the language barrier. Mr. Sinh seemed to realize that Viet did not understand what he said. He took him to the black board in the Living room that had a bunch of writing on it, including the big heading "House Rules." They both stared at the board for a while as Mr. Sinh did his best to explain the rules using sign language. Viet tried to listen carefully and understand. Mr. Sinh then took Viet and a handful of new kids to another house nearby called the Clothing Center of the camp to get some clothes and shoes for them. Viet was not quite sure where they were heading, but after the doors of the Center were open, he knew immediately what the place was. They could take as many items as they needed. Viet could not believe all the shirts, jeans, socks, shoes, sandals, and so on that were available. He had never seen that much stuff in his life! He thought he died and ended up in clothing heaven.

This experience reminded Viet of the Bible story about Joseph and his family after their reconciliation. Joseph took his brothers to the grain storage and let them take home whatever they needed to survive the drought. His brothers' jaws must have dropped when they were shown all the storage bins. They must have been overwhelmed by the amount of grain (Genesis 45:20-23). Viet took a bunch of clothes, socks, sandals, and shoes back to his orphanage house.

Before long, it was lunch time, and everyone was summoned to the dining room for a meal together. Everyone lined up on both sides of a long buffet table and scooped their portions from different dishes to their own plates. Viet never saw anything like that before. It looked almost like a production assembly line—like something he saw in a factory. Back home, if there was a big family gathering with many people, everyone sat at different tables where food was served to them. The lunch buffet was something new to him. But, that was not the only new thing he experienced on his first meal in the new world. He had to pick up a fork, knife, spoon, napkin, and tray at one end of the buffet table and learn how to use them properly during the meal. He also had to keep track of his three-course meal, namely, salad or appetizer, main dish, and dessert. In his home country, all he had to worry about was having food on the table for a meal. If he was lucky, he had some fruit for dessert at home. Obviously, this was just the beginning of a long learning process with big adjustments that Viet had to go through in the new culture.

People might take these little things of their daily life for granted. But, a refugee or an immigrant must struggle through these and many other issues just to stay alive. The meal etiquette, along with many Western customs and a new language, was what Viet had to learn during the five months he spent in Camp Freedom. In the upcoming days, he attended several classes on various topics and tried to prepare himself for his new life in the Western world.

Viet did not know how many houses there were in the camp yet, but each house was assigned to different tasks to keep the camp running smoothly 24/7. One house helped with cooking in the kitchen, while another helped clean up the dining room. One house was assigned to keep the whole camp clean, while another maintained the school building and its classrooms neat and tidy. Everyone in the camp had to sign up and attend a language class, a cultural class, and a few other classes several times a week. In exchange, the United Nations High Commissioner for Refugees (UNHCR) compensated them by giving them three dollars a week for personal use. That might not sound like much for most Westerners and their high living standard. But, for refugees who left everything behind in their home countries and had nothing besides a shirt on their back, it was like manna from Heaven. That amount was like striking oil or winning a big jackpot. Everyone in Camp Freedom was very thankful for the financial help as they tried to make it through day by day.

Viet might not have supported and agreed with everything that the United Nations did over the years and its messy politics. However, its involvement with refugees and protecting the most vulnerable was something Viet experienced first-hand, and he highly commended the organization for that great work. He appreciated everything the whole world did for him to help him stay alive with that little financial assistance each week. This positive experience was part of a long process that helped Viet realize the importance of reaching out and giving a hand to the misfortunate and those in need.

People who look down on refugees or mistreat them do not realize that Jesus was once a refugee. When a person does not welcome a refugee, he or she does not welcome Jesus either. The Bible tells us that when Joseph—the foster father of Jesus—received a message from an angel about the upcoming massacre of infants by King Herod, he took the entire Holy Family and escaped to Egypt overnight (Matthew 2:13-15). Jesus and His family hid in Egypt until King Herod died before they returned to their homeland. Imagine if the Egyptian authorities had decided to keep the Holy Family out of its country? Where would they have gone? They might have fallen victim to the evil King Herod. Is that what we would want to happen to Jesus? Do we really want to treat the Son of God and our Savior that way? When we become envious of refugees and fear they will take our jobs and drain our resources, we feel the same toward Jesus. When we do not have compassion and care for refugees, we treat Jesus the same way. Even though we might be in better shape than the refugees in every way, some of us still act selfishly and want them to have nothing. That is terrible and unchristian! It would be extremely sad to see a Christian or an American act in such a way toward a helpless refugee. Besides, if we look back in our own family lines, we must admit that we were all refugees at one time.

Viet experienced the life of a refugee in a camp for quite some time and knew what a refugee must endure first-hand. That personal experience helped him be a humble and compassionate person in dealing with refugees or other human beings. Most of us do not realize the pain and concern that a refugee endures. Foremost, a refugee struggles with the language barrier and the ability to understand and communicate with others. Most people do not know how painful and frustrating it is for a refugee to be unable to express his or her true feelings and understand what others say. But, that is not the only thing a refugee faces. One does not know what tomorrow might bring. At a camp, one cannot figure out which country might grant him or her asylum or how one's future might turn out. One might get stuck in a refugee camp for a long time because of paperwork and bureaucracy. In fact, some people had been in Camp Freedom for a decade. They must have felt hopeless and frustrated. Worse yet, a refugee does not have much except a shirt on his or her back and a few belongings. It is pathetic for anyone to feel jealous or threatened that a refugee might succeed or beat him or her financially. It takes hard work and a long time before that would ever happen. A refugee must motivate him- or herself to wake up every day and find a reason to live despite the huge mountain of challenges laid before him or her. Still, refugees are always hopeful and thankful to be alive because of the grace of God.

Like most successful refugees, Viet had to work harder than normal people and rely on divine help to guide and protect him from his very first day in the refugee camp. After helping clean up the dining room, he was asked to keep the orphanage house clean as well. Mr. Sinh specifically warned him and every kid in the house to put trash in the waste basket and not spit gum on the floor. The orphanage house leader hated that and would punish the guilty severely. In case anyone does not know, Singapore is an extremely clean country. It gave people a big fine—more than a couple of hundred dollars, or put someone in jail if one was caught littering. This country also had great cuisine and high living standards. It attracted many tourists and retirees from around the world including the USA, Australia, and New Zealand. Some of them volunteered to teach English and custom classes at Camp Freedom. All the members of the camp certainly appreciated those priceless volunteers and their wonderful contributions. Yet, the accent of the volunteers from Australia and New Zeeland made it quite interesting for these refugees to learn English. That did not even include their various slang and traditional sayings. The English class was never boring, and this refugee camp was really like a miniature model of the United Nations. Everyone in the camp needed to attend classes in the morning, and they had the afternoon and evening free.

However, that portion of the day was not really free. One often used that time to line up at the business office and collect his or her weekly pay or meet with the United Nations representatives or the consults of various countries for endless interviews and vetting process before being accepted by a country. Viet often used the afternoon to complete his assigned cleaning duty in the dining room and the house. Before long, the entire afternoon was over and everyone was ready for dinner in the early evening. Viet and some of his housemates had to do the cleaning for the dining room all over again. It was a productive, busy, and overwhelming first day at Camp Freedom. He could not wait to go back to his bunkbed in the Orphanage House and call it a day. This was his first night at the camp and on land since his escape from Viet Nam. Although he was emotionally and mentally exhausted, he could not close his eyes. He stared at the ceiling and thought about his time and journey away from home. He could not believe that it has been almost a month since the moment he left his home country. It was also the first time he slept safely on land and not floating at sea. He was so thankful for that blessing and realized that his presence at Camp Freedom was truly a miracle. He knew that his loving God had protected him and brought him safely to this foreign land despite all the dangers and hardships along the way. His body could lay at the bottom of the sea or get stranded on some deserted island instead of this bunkbed.

Suddenly, he felt all alone for the first time and missed home. He did not know where he would go from here and was completely overwhelmed by the language barrier and all the new things he had to learn in a new country. Although his father was already in the USA, he did not bring along his address or phone number to contact because he feared that he would be in lots of troubles if the Communists had caught him. The only thing he brought with him and was still in his pocket was some ginger. This homemade and traditional remedy was used effectively to deal with seasickness and as a sign of the constant presence of his ancestors throughout the harrowing journey. That special root reminded him home even more and made him wonder when he would be able to be able to see them all again. When he thought about it, tears began to roll down his cheeks. He did not know what else to do except to pray for them and hope that his loving God would continue to watch over them and perform lots of miracles in their lives like He has done for him. Between prayers and the overwhelming feeling of homesickness, Viet slowly fell asleep and go his much-needed rest.

He was awakened by an announcement broadcasted over the loudspeakers throughout the camp. He was warmly greeted by the beautiful sunshine of a new day. Although he did not want to get out of bed due to his fear of an overwhelming burden of life and a depressing feeling of loneliness, Viet had to push himself to be a strong believer and an eternal optimist and get on with this beautiful day. Besides, a goodnight's sleep did ease some of his worries and restored his strength to continue with his life journey. What many people do not know is that a refugee must rely on God for help. For he or she does not have anyone else to rely on. A refugee also must be the most hopeful person. He or she cannot go on and make it through another day without being an eternal optimist. Finally, a refugee must learn to get along with everyone wherever he or she goes to survive. If he or she constantly agitates others and creates fights with people around him or her, he or she will not make it far along his or her life. A refugee must learn to get along with everyone around, trust in God above everything else, and be hopeful even in the darkest moments of his or her life.

Like the rest of the camp, Viet tried to go on with his daily routine and make the best out of his life in the camp. How his future might turn out and where he might end up in the days ahead, he would need to put it in God's hands. Every day he had his three meals, attended the required classes, took care of his assigned duties, and began to explore the camp and its host country a little more. He went around the camp to introduce himself and get to know all his neighbors. He made new friends and tried to create a normal life for himself on this foreign land. He learned that Camp Freedom used to be a British basic training camp. The current houses for refugees were the barracks for English soldiers. The whole camp took a huge area and there were certain parts of it that all the refugees were warned to keep off. Everyone could contact their loved ones throughout the world by mail only. There was no phone or fax for anyone to communicate with his or her family and friends. Viet was so happy and thankful about that permission.

Now, he could contact his family and see where God might send him too. Hopefully, it would not be back to Viet Nam. But, without the address of his father who was granted political asylum in the USA for working with the American GI's or the contact information of some of his relatives who lived in France, Viet had to write back home to get all that information. He could not carry along anything of that kind for fear of being caught by the Communists and punished severely for it. Now, he had to take a chance to write home and ask for it. Otherwise, he would be stuck at the camp for a long time or sent back to Viet Nam for having no sponsorship. But, by contacting his family, he might put them in jeopardy if the Communists opened his letter and found out where he might be. Or, his letter might be intercepted by the authorities and would never be delivered to his family at all. Anyone who had never dealt with the Communists should know they are cunning, crafty, deceptive, devious, evil, ruthless, authoritarian, undemocratic, and censorial. They could open, check on, and confiscate anything they wanted. Besides, it would take almost a month for his letter to get home and another month for anything to get back to him. Despite those challenges, Viet had no choice and decided to write back home to request the necessary contact information of his father and other relatives. All he could do after that was to pray and hope for the best. But, before he sealed that letter and sent it out, Viet thought about their plight and difficulties of living under a Communist government. He decided to enclose all the money he had for his family back home, including all the Vietnamese currencies that he brought along during his escape. He could not turn a blind eye on their misfortunes and simply live for himself. Rather, he had tried all his life to live for Jesus and others and learned to have a generous and caring heart. This focus for his life has given him strength to face various challenges and reason to keep moving forward each day.

While Viet patiently waited for the response of his letter, he visited many other camp members and listened to their harrowing stories. Most of them were extremely sad and made Viet's long journey seem like a walk in Disney Land. For example, a dozen of people in a barrack said that their boat of almost a hundred people was stranded at sea almost two months without being rescued by any ship at all. They started out with plenty of supplies and foods and thought that they could go around the world without any problem. Unfortunately, they chased one ship after another whenever they spotted something on the horizon. They zigzagged from one corner of the earth to another and ran into all sorts of weather conditions and problems. They soon ran out of everything and just waited for death. Some of their weak members slowly died and, before long, half of their boat was dead. The members who were lucky enough to be alive had to make a tough decision on whether they would eat their dead boat mates to live a bit longer or not. It took them a few days to consider that. Meanwhile, some more of them died off.

Evidently, there were just a couple of dozens of them left in the end. But, only half of them would choose to eat the dead to stay alive. They described how gross and gruesome it was for them to cut off a piece of another human being and swallow it whole. They had to block out all their senses and tried to think about what they were doing, except their survival. They threw up plenty of times and had to convince themselves that they had no other choice other than trying to stay alive. That experience forever changed their lives, but they were so thankful to be alive. As they shared this awful experience with Viet, tears rolled down their cheeks slowly. They also mumbled the names of the deceased that they ate, "I'm sorry... Duyen,...Hanh,... Thuy,...Van,...Long,...Duc,...Dung,..." However, they did not behave differently compared to everyone else in the camp. Viet and his boat mates were very close to experiencing the same thing if the divine miracle of being rescued by the South Korean ship has not come to pass. Viet tried to comfort these folks and give them some messages of hope before he left.

Stories of cannibalism were not the only tragic stories that Viet heard around the camp. Another day, Viet stopped by the barrack near the entrance of the camp for a visit and picked up another horrible story from a group of women. They had survived horrible pirate attacks. They looked normal on the outside like the rest of folks in the camp, but deep down these women carried deep pain and tried to carry on with their lives without taking it out on others or becoming cynical in dealing with the world. They told Viet that they had to rely on the power from above to help them deal with the pain of this wound and keep on living for their families and friends back home. They thought that they were spared and left alive by the pirates for a reason. They did not want that traumatic experience to scare them from living or turn them into bitter and depressed people. Rather, they would like to show the world their purpose to keep on living.

Apparently, their boat was captured by pirates several times and all their supplies and possessions were taken away. Each pirate attack became worse. The first time they ran into a group of pirates who took only their valuable possessions and supplies and let them go after pushing them around a little bit. The second time they encountered pirates, their treatment was worse than the first. They apparently got rubbed up really good. The pirates beat up the men and raped the women. Several of their boat mates lost their lives. Perhaps they came across to their attackers as a bit too annoying. The dead corpses were tossed overboard. That ruthless act was perhaps designed to intimidate and scare the boatful of refugees from putting up further resistance. But, the pirates' barbaric act toward the dead corpses had a much deeper effect than they might think. It horrified and traumatized all the survivors, who were raised in a traditional and respectful culture toward the dead. Still, they all were not ready to see the pirates kidnap some of their boat mates and speed off. Unfortunately, that was not the last time these unfortunate folks ran into pirates. Another group of pirates came along and murdered additional people in this boat after robbing them of whatever they had left. A handful of survivors were lucky to be left alive. They somehow managed to make it through those terrible ordeals and were later rescued by a foreign ship.

Viet shed tears just listening to their horrific story and quietly gave thanks to God for sparing him from the same nightmare. He gave these few courageous souls a firm handshake, wished them all the best with their new lives in the camp, and bid them farewell before leaving that courageous barrack.

Viet continued to live each day in Camp Freedom with joy and hope and tried to get to know as many camp residents as he could. It seemed as if everyone had a story to tell. Most of them had immense emotional bruises and deep psychological scars from their escape journeys. None of them made it to the camp without some sort of emotional wound. They even shared with Viet many stories of missing relatives and friends who were presumed dead, but their bodies were never found. Many missing refugees ended up drowning at sea, and some of them drifted to God-forsaken islands. Very few were later found and rescued. Meanwhile, more than a dozen of the camp's residents had been there for many years. They had no relatives in the free world to sponsor them. Neither were they accepted by one of the

Western countries. Although the Viet Nam War and persecution by the oppressive Communist regime motivated many Vietnamese to escape and be granted political asylum, not all of them were fortunate enough to have had that wish come true. Most Western countries required a refugee to have a sponsoring relative or friend with residency in their country before allowing them to enter. The only two countries that had a liberal policy of accepting refugees were Canada and France.

While Viet talked to some camp residents who had been there for years, reality began to set in for him, and he started to worry if he might turn out to be one of them. It had been more than a month since the day Viet sent a letter home to ask for his father's address in the USA and other relatives' contact information in other Western countries. Today, he had a pleasant surprise and received a letter from home. All the money—Vietnamese currencies and US dollars—he sent home surprisingly were received and now he had the necessary address to contact his father and other relatives. He was so happy and thankful to be able to get in touch with his father and family members.

But, he was not completely out of the woods yet. He still had to meet with the United Nations and the US officials for the vetting process. He had to go through half a dozen meetings with those officials to figure out if he was a legitimate refugee and whether he would be granted a permit to enter the US. The vetting process was always brutal for a refugee, partly because of the language barrier and the series of difficult and stressful questions. A refugee was asked about his or her family, life under the Communists, reasons for leaving his or her home country, details about his or her persecution, purposes for coming to America, names and contact information of family and friends in America, the ability of his or her family and friends to take care of the refugee, and so on. Each refugee had to meet with the interviewers of his or her destination country and the United Nations at least half a dozen of times before any decision was made about his or her acceptance status into that country. Only the lucky ones were granted asylum in various countries around the world, while the unlucky ones were stuck in the camp indefinitely and could ultimately face deportation.

For someone who does not know what a refugee must deal with daily or how life in a refugee camp was, the best way Viet could describe or compare it is like living in Limbo or Purgatory. Christians used this theological concept to explain the fate of unbaptized babies or Christians with minor sins after this life. They would be stuck in Limbo or Purgatory while waiting for their chance to get to Heaven. Like Limbo or Purgatory, a refugee camp is a holding place where a refugee waits for his or her chance to be accepted into a Western country. His or her life is basically on hold indefinitely, and he or she must rely on the mercy and care of other human beings, namely the interviewers, to help him or her to move out of the refugee camp.

Camp life is somewhat like being in prison. It has curfew, restrictions, and all sorts of rules and regulations. Its members are cut off from the rest of the world and limited regarding what they can do. Food and necessities are provided, but they are not the best. Otherwise, everyone would want to stay in the refugee camp instead of moving on! Although life in Camp Freedom might feel like being Limbo or Purgatory at times, Viet and all the residents there did their best to cherish every moment and learn to share it generously with everyone around. He hung out with visitors and took field trips with them to check out Singapore when it was allowed. There were some visitors who came from America, Australia, New Zealand, and so on to volunteer their time to tutor the refugees in English and Western culture and customs in the camp.

Viet remembered a young Vietnamese who was a student at the University of Berkley in California came to help at the camp for several months. One day he saw a group of young refugee men walk with their arms across each other's shoulders. He quickly pulled them aside and told them to stop doing that to avoid any misunderstanding in the new culture. Back home that casual act might be considered acceptable among friends. But, in Western culture, that friendly act might communicate to others that the entire group of young men was gay. Another visitor that stood out for Viet at the camp was Mr. Tan. He was a middle-aged, single man who made his living as an engineer and was a citizen of Singapore. He felt sympathetic to the children in the Orphanage House and came by the camp weekly to take them for a tour of the city or some fun activities. Each camp member could leave the camp once a week on a certain time and day. A person could go shopping and enjoy the city by taking a bus, but could not get a job and work outside of the camp. Surely, there were curfew and other camp rules and regulations that all its members had to follow. Otherwise, they would incur punishment and other severe penalties, including deportation.

Mr. Tan often came to visit us and took the entire Orphanage House out for dinner, shopping, swimming, and so on. He would let us drive his car on the left lane inside the camp to see how weird that would feel compared to the opposite way in America and other places around the world. Singapore was a British colony at one point, and the United Kingdom had some influences on its customs and lifestyle. Mr. Tan's kind and generous act not only touched everyone in the Orphanage House deeply but also helped them make it through those tough days in a refugee camp. Viet was one of the children who no longer felt lonesome or abandoned in that house. He also brought the love of God to everyone in the camp and helped them make some good memories out of a sad and tough situation. He reminded the whole camp that there were plenty of good people like him out there in the world.

Sometimes, our dark, cunning world might make us assume that everyone is bad and evil like the pirates or the Communists. But, God does send good people our way every day to give us a hand and lift our spirits. They also help encourage us to be like them and try to live each day for our Creator and others around us. That is the best and only way for us to change our world for the better and give good purpose for our lives. When we can live for something bigger than us, our lives will be filled with joy and satisfaction, and we will not regret wasting our lives in the end. Viet would always be grateful to people like Mr. Tan for all the wonderful things he did for the orphans and refugees in Camp Freedom.

Because of Mr. Tan's great example, Viet committed himself to live each day for his Lord Jesus and others. Kind and generous deeds like Mr. Tan's also made time in the camp go faster and before long Viet made contact with his father in the USA. A few weeks after that, he received the exciting news about his departure from the camp for the USA.

Singapore was certainly a spectacular country with good food, clean streets, high technology, a great living standard, and dedicated people. Like many Asian countries, it has a bargaining system for buying and selling things at stores and outdoor markets. Many of its stores were set up alongside the streets so that shoppers could walk from one store to the next with ease. It also has a whole mall designated for food so people could walk from one booth of food to the next for several neighborhood blocks. It surely has many awesome sites for the world's visitors to see. Viet would be forever grateful to Singapore for welcoming refugees and camp volunteers around the world who sacrificed time and resources to care for the lowly and the outcast.

At the end of the summer, Viet was permitted to enter the USA under his father's sponsorship. He spent almost six months in Camp Freedom in Singapore and gained a unique and invaluable experience about life and humanity from the perspective of a refugee. He can assure anyone who might have any concern or worry about refugees that 99.99 percent of all refugees are good, sincere people. These folks, for one reason or another, had to leave behind everything, including their families and friends, and risked their lives for the dream of a new life or, in Viet's case, a life of freedom. Anyone who is envious of a refugee and afraid of what he or she might lose to a refugee is not only pathetic but also uncaring for the lowly and the outcast.

A refugee comes to a new land with empty hands, a hardworking ethic, and a hopeful spirit. A refugee also must deal with hardships right from the beginning, including a language barrier and past hurts and suffering. Viet listened to many painful stories from other refugees in the camp and could relate to them well personally. The unique experience and his living with the Communists after the Viet Nam War made Viet real to the world and softened his heart to the plight of the lowly and the suffering. Viet was also moved by the kindness and generosity of the many volunteers who reached out to the forgotten refugees in Camp Freedom and did their best to lift the spirits of these broken and abandoned souls. The refugee camp experience made Viet much more compassionate to suffering and pushed him to become more like his Savior Jesus. He vowed to live for his Lord Jesus and others and try to help the lowly as much as possible.

Viet left Camp Freedom one morning with two small suitcases full of good memories and gratitude. He also made friends with some people at the camp. His plane made its first stop in Thailand, then Tokyo for some fuel before landing in San Francisco late evening of the day before he actually left Singapore (an eight-hour difference). He could not kiss the ground of this dream land, but said a prayer of thanksgiving the moment he landed in America.

Chapter 10

The Promised Land: Dream and Reality

Viet's plane landed in San Francisco at night and he finally arrived at his dream land safely. He tried to look out the window of the plane to have a first glimpse of this strange land. This was the moment he had been dreaming about all his life. However, under the dimming, yellowish light of the street and parking lamps, all he could see was lots of concrete and some brownish grass. He also noticed how vast everything was in the dream land compared to his homeland or Singapore. It seemed like his homeland was much more crowded than the dream land.

Viet had read a lot about America in story books and other literature since sixth grade as he tried to learn English. He picked up new words and built his vocabulary by reading stories such as Cinderella, Jack and the Beanstalk, Snow White, Little Red Riding Hood, the Ugly Duckling, Sleeping Beauty, the Three Little Pigs, Rumpelstiltskin, Goldilocks and the Three Bears, Hansel and Gretel, Beauty and the Beast, Aladdin, and so on. Those stories excited his imagination and took him to fairytale lands that he often associated with America. For Viet, America was the land where all wonderful things could happen for anyone who dared to dream.

Foremost, it is the land of freedom and opportunities. Everyone is free to live one's own lifestyle, worship the way one feels is suitable, eat and drink anything one likes, listen to one's own favorite music and radio programs, watch the news and any show one enjoys, travel wherever and whenever one desires, elect one's own chosen officials, and so on. That sounds like a Heavenly place, where everyone would love to come and make a home. If someone has ever lived in a Communist or dictatorship country like Viet did, he or she would recognize a Heavenly place when he or she sees it. Anyone would be thankful for it and cherish it once he or she has a taste of the land of freedom and opportunities.

In a Communist country, everyone must dress, look, and live the way the government demands. Viet recalled that all students had to even have their fingernails cut short, even the girls. The boys had to have their haircut a certain way. He witnessed every day how some of his schoolmates were disciplined for having their hair or fingernails too long. A few times, he even witnessed his classmates have their heads shaved in the middle of the whole class and humiliated for not obeying the Communist rules. All students also had to wear a red dude rag around their neck to honor the Communist government and its leader, Uncle Ho. Many students did not like that imposing red dude rag and often put it in their pocket. And, students were not the only group the Communists tried to control. Right from the beginning, the Communists banned the public from wearing any clothing with Western logos or American advertising messages. They did not allow citizens to listen to Western music, the British Broadcasting Corporation (BBC), or Voice of America (VOA). Some people were jailed for listening to one of these forbidden Western stations. The government also discouraged and threatened women who wanted their fingernails painted. If discovered, the Communists would pull their nails out.

But, like anything forbidden, people tended to do the opposite and violate forbidden things a lot more. People would dress, wear, listen, consume, read, and basically live the way they liked regardless of the consequences. They also kept attending Christian churches and Buddhist temples weekly, if not daily, to worship and pray, even though the Communist authorities continued to watch and discourage them from gathering in big groups and practicing their religious beliefs. The government also made each family display the Communist flag and a picture of its leader, Uncle Ho, inside their homes and pledge allegiance to it instead of some god in one's religion.

Viet recalled pointing to the picture of Uncle Ho as a child and asking his family, "Who is that?" Later, he saw the picture of Uncle Ho everywhere he went, including classrooms, shops, stores, worship places, offices, street corners, and so on. He soon realized Uncle Ho was the leader of the Vietnamese Communist movement. He also learned that the Communists required all travelers to ask for a permit before going from one town to the next. Worst of all, the authority controlled all the supplies and made daily life miserable for everyone. Everything was always in short supply. Some daily things such as sugar could not be stocked up over a certain amount. One could be jailed for having too much of some daily supplies in one's house. There was a widespread shortage of all kinds of necessities every week. There were also not a lot of choices for most consumer items. All in all, life with the Communists was tough. Everything was dark, gloomy, and hopeless for its citizens.

While dealing with a dead-end life in a Communist country, Viet discovered a new world in America through story books and other literature. He thought America was like a fairy land with lots of wonderful things and amazing people. Viet pictured Americans as big, tall, talented, resilient, strong, handsome folks with a strong sense of justice and a generous spirit. They will always stand up to anything unjust and evil in the world and defeat it without any hesitation like he read about in many classic stories. They take on the mantle of justice and defend the weak and the poor against the powerful and the wicked. They give generously to the needy and reach out to the misfortunate. Most of Viet's images of Americans came from story books. Some of those images include Robin Hood in English folklore, Jack in *Jack and the Beanstalk*, or Snow White in *Snow White*. Those evidently were American heroes who stood up for justice and defended the weak against an unfair and evil system of governance.

They were surely the source of inspiration for Viet and other oppressed folks around the world. They were like knights on white horses who risked their lives and reputation to defend the oppressed and take care of the poor. They helped bring freedom and justice to the world. That is what Viet and many folks around the world have looked for from America. Freedom and justice are like diamonds and hidden treasures that the whole world has tried to find its daily life. The world has gone to the ends of the earth and looked in every country to search for those gifts, but has come away empty handed. But, it cannot give up just yet on that search. Day after day, the world has wrestled with itself in search of the greatest treasures of all—freedom and justice—and thankfully has been able to find those qualities in America.

Viet lived under the Communist system, which had very little regard for the ideas of freedom and justice and their importance in the lives of citizens. Without freedom to think, voice an opinion, worship, gather, travel, live, and choose a certain way of life, a person feels like an animal living in a cage. But, that was how Viet and his countrymen had to endure silently. They had to live a life without freedom for years and felt as if they had nowhere to go with their lives. They felt confined and hopeless under the Communist regime. They looked to America where freedom has become the air that its citizens breathe daily. Everyone in America lives freely and dreams big. Viet had read about America and considered it the Promised Land, where he would have total freedom to live and pursue his dreams. He could think freely without being controlled by the Communist doctrines. He could speak freely without being jailed for his personal opinions or feelings about an issue. He could gather for a meeting or worship without being threatened with arrest. He could travel from one town to another city and visit someone he liked without having to ask for government permission. Best of all, he could live his life in his own way without being penalized for it. He truly appreciated the gift of freedom and understood well the slogan of the State of New Hampshire—one of the fifty states in the United States of America—Live free or die. Our lives would not be the same without the gift of freedom.

Another gift Viet found in America was justice. He read a lot about Justice in stories such as Robin Hood, Jack and the Beanstalk, or Snow White and the Seven Dwarfs. In the Robin Hood story, Viet loved the fact that a hero like Robin Hood could rescue the poor and the oppressed and stand up to the rich and the powerful. Robin Hood dared to put his life on the line and deliver justice. He helped people find fairness and hope in an evil, difficult world. He represented hope and salvation that the lowly and the weak had been praying for. Viet also appreciated the courageous and adventurous figure of Jack in the story of Jack and the Beanstalk. Like many heroic figures in classic stories, life dealt him a bad hand, and everything seemed to stack up against him. But, instead of feeling depressed and cursing his misfortune, Jack kept venturing out into the world and making good use of what he had until he found a great treasure up in Heaven. Even though that treasure fully belonged to him, Jack learned to share it with his loved ones. He captured, for Viet, a sense of justice and adventure in all Americans and called others to think outside of the box and do the same. His resiliency in a difficult time was something else that Viet admired about the character of Jack. Like many Vietnamese and people who faced daily challenges around the world, Viet looked up to heroic figures like Jack to help him overcome adversities and find a solution for his problems. Viet certainly found similar inspiration in the character Snow White in the story of Snow White and the Seven Dwarfs. This story shows us the real human drama that happens around us every day. An evil queen tries to hurt and oppress the lowly and the just. She thinks she can get away with her devious act and everything will turn out the way she wants. But, God does not let her wicked deeds go unnoticed and sends the seven dwarfs to help Snow White. Eventually, Snow White finds a happy life with Prince Charming and runs far away from the evil queen.

Surely, freedom and justice are two important, shining values that Viet found in many American classic stories. For years, Americans have stood up for the weak and have fought against oppressors and evil powers around the world. Sometimes, those fights for justice might look messy and cause lots of collateral damage to the innocent. But, overall America has been the defender of justice, lover of freedom, and beacon of hope for the lowly and the oppressed. Our world would not be the same if America did not stand up against evil leaders and the power of darkness in the name of justice. America must commit itself to be the promoter and defender of justice for the whole world at all costs if the people of good will have a chance to defeat evil and darkness. The day that America gives up on the fights against evil and darkness or gets tired of defending justice will be the day the beacon of hope and goodness will get dimmed drastically. Eventually, that light will disappear, and the power of evil and darkness will take complete control of the earth. Acts of injustice and oppression will sadly be the only thing one will find on the face of the earth. That is why Viet had admired America for what it has stood for and done for the world.

Freedom and justice are great values that America has stood for. Besides these spectacular attributes, Viet had viewed America from the other side of the ocean as the wonderful land of opportunities, dreams, and hopes. He learned from history that people left Europe and four corners of the world to come to America to achieve their dreams. Columbus did not risk his life and go on a dangerous voyage to get stuck in the old world. Rather, he took on that difficult journey because he wanted to dream of a great new world. He hoped to discover a new land and begin to build new dreams there. He wanted to leave behind the old life and all its suffering and persecution. Since the time of Columbus, there have been thousands of migrants who have made America their homeland and started to dream about their new lives there. The early settlers had to run from all the persecution in their home countries and hoped to dream big in the new land. Many of them suffered from religious persecution, while others did not have economic opportunities in their homeland due to the tight control of the ruling class. They did everything in their power to come to America and often risked their own lives for it. They worked hard from the first moment they set foot on the new land, and began to dream the impossible in this country. They surely encountered all sorts of difficulties along the way, but never stopped dreaming and pushing themselves to achieve the impossible. Over time, they have been able to make their dreams come true and create new opportunities for others around them.

This wave of dreamers is what made America great and continues to help it build success upon success. There have been thousands of successful stories from migrants and immigrants who came to America with nothing and began to build their dream businesses from the ground up. After they have successfully created their business franchises, they do not collect their profits, roll up their businesses, and turn around to go back home. Rather, they invest their profits into their old businesses and create new ones so that others may get inspired and start their own. That is how this great country has been built and hopefully will remain an incubator of dreams and opportunities for future generations of Americans. America is certainly the land for dreamers and risk takers. If someone dares to dream—big and small alike—he or she has a place in the land of America and can help it build a shining city on the hill that would be an envy of the world. If someone can capitalize on all the opportunities that America provides him or her, he or she should be welcomed to be a part of American society and help create other opportunities for future generations. This is what Viet loves and appreciates about America.

All the talk lately about closing the borders and limiting the number of refugees coming into America not only goes contrary to the Christian virtue of charity, but also undermines the essential principles on which America was founded such as liberty, justice, equality, and the pursue of happiness. Christian values were surely the bedrock from which the founding fathers and mothers build up the America that we have now. Furthermore, America has been the land of dreams and hopes for people from all walks of life. By closing the borders and limiting the number of refugees coming here, we would say to the world that we do not need any more dreamers or our dreams are better than others. Either way we would limit our possibilities to thrive and grow as a nation. Any country that does not create dreams and hope for its people, but only looks inward, will kill its people slowly and eventually wither and die. Viet experienced firsthand in his birth country how the Communist government killed the dreams and hope of the people by limiting opportunities for them to develop and by controlling new ideas. The result of this bad, short-sighted policy is that its people have suffered in misery and many of them have abandoned it and sought new opportunities to prosper somewhere else. Viet wondered, "Is that what we want America to become?"

Another great value that Viet loved about America is the idea of competition. This fantastic idea challenges status quo and complacency and calls on everyone to work hard and become innovative to succeed in America. It eliminates laziness and keeps society moving forward. When two sports teams compete, they show genuine respect to each other and hold each other accountable for all their actions. They challenge each other to work hard for fear that they might let down their coaches and fans. They help each other come up with new ways to do things better. Competition makes things fun and at the same time gives people lots of choices. Any society that promotes competition is never boring.

Unfortunately, Viet had lived in a Communist society without much competition at all. Its core principle was about taking care of the common good and ignoring individual needs. Everyone had to sacrifice themselves for the sake of the common good. No one could get ahead of others and leave some people behind. There was no individual possession. Everything one has in a Communist country belongs to the whole society. Because of its lack of competition, no one has any incentive to work harder or come up with new ideas to make things better. For everything is owned by the whole society, or the Communist government to be exact. There was no competition under the Communist rule, and everything became stagnant, boring, unproductive, and dead. There was no growth, excitement, or innovation when individuals were not encouraged to compete. Everyone would simply do the same thing in the exact same manner every day and try not to rock the boat. Everything is boring and dead in a noncompetitive society. No one really wants America to become like that.

Other wonderful qualities the world admires about America are its generosity, kindness, and caring. All the classic American stories that Viet read revealed these qualities repeatedly. For example, in the fabulous tale of the Little Red Riding Hood, Viet was amazed by the kindness and caring that Little Red showed to her grandma in a cunning and devious world. That world was represented by a selfish, mean, and deceptive wolf. All the wolf cared about was itself and its needs. It went as far as eating Little Red's grandma and hoping to do the same to her to satisfy its needs. Still, Little Red continued to show her kindness and caring in the face of that selfish and devious world. Perhaps she was a bit naïve, but she showed the world and Viet what America truly stands for regardless of how things might look like around it. America will always be generous, kind, and caring to the world.

But, that is not the only story that shows the adorable qualities about America. Another classic fable that underscored this was Goldilocks and the Three Bears. This cute story tells the tale about Goldilocks' little adventure that led her to the cozy cabin of the three bears—the father, the mother, and the baby—while its owners were not home. Goldilocks made herself at home and ate three bowls of soup without any hesitation and then laid down in their beds. Eventually, the three bears came home and quickly learned that there was an intruder in their home who ate their soup and slept in their beds. They could have become furious and gone to the ends of earth to search for that perpetrator and make him or her pay for it. But, the story did not end that way. Viet took it as a calling and challenge for him and the whole world to be kind, caring, and generous. This is what America is all about. While Viet was still thousands of miles away from America, he admired these wonderful attributes about America among many other great ones and dreamed about making it to that Promised Land someday.

Viet was not the only one who cherished and desired the fine attributes of generosity and kindness proudly demonstrated in America—the greatest nation on earth. Many holy figures in Christian tradition have practiced and promoted these fantastic virtues. They have tried their best to live a life of love and kindness. They have pushed themselves to be kind and loving not only to their neighbors but also their enemies. This level of kindness and love is something one can only find in God. "For God lets the sun rise on the bad and the good, and causes rain fall on the just and the unjust." (Matthew 5:45) These holy figures have also called on others and challenged themselves to be perfect like their God and show generosity to the world beyond their own boundaries. Most of them have made personal sacrifices, including offering their own lives for a higher purpose, namely, their Lord Jesus Christ and the Kingdom of Heaven. Their belief in the value of generosity and kindness have brought wonderful changes to themselves and life-giving transformations to the world. Our world would not be the same if those holy Christian figures had not yearned for and promoted the virtues of generosity and kindness. Many lives around the world have reaped great benefits from the generosity and kindness of such holy Christians. Similarly, many folks in many parts of the world have been blessed by the generosity and kindness of Americans over the years.

It is sad for Viet to see some Americans recently have become selfish and want their country to turn inward. That short-sighted thinking will pitch America against the whole world and tarnish its great image in the eyes of others. Also, as the result, the whole world might no longer see America as the shining city on the hill and the finest example of generosity and kindness for other people to emulate. Unfortunately, selfishness and mean spiritedness will only produce negative consequences. Viet is a strong believer in being generous and kind to others as the basic code of conduct for one's daily living. Indeed, the more a person gives, the more one will receive in return. In fact, Viet's entire life journey has been the result of many generous and kind benefactors. These folks have extended their hands and helped him in many ways, especially in times of need. Without them, he could not deal with all his life challenges, and he would not be here now. He is forever in debt to them and his loving God.

Chapter 11

Searching for a New Identity and Life Mission
in the New World

The hardest thing for a refugee in a new world is not about leaving behind his or her family, friends, and everything else of the old world. Rather, it is his or her adjustment into a new culture. He or she must learn the new language, eat strange food, make new friends, and get accustomed to all the strange customs. We take for granted our ability to communicate and understand the language of the land, namely, English, with ease. We can tell someone what we want and express to others how we truly feel about something without any problem. We have no trouble picking up what people want to talk to us about every day. We do not have to search our brains to figure out when people try to tell us something. But, a refugee must struggle with all this every day, at least in the beginning. He or she cannot understand what people say to him or her. Neither can he or she respond and communicate to others. A refugee can easily become isolated and lonely due to the language barrier.

Viet could totally relate to everything shared above about the life of a refugee in the new land. For he could not talk or understand people around him and had to spend many restless nights crying in bed. He felt frustrated and hopeless like a mute and a deaf. He remembered that, in the beginning, there were times that people greeted him, "How are you doing?" and he knew how to respond to this question, namely, "I'm fine, thank you." But, he found himself stumble through the answer and try to spit out those simple words in the right order. Before he got the answer clearly expressed, the other person unfortunately was long gone. This stumbling problem continued to happen and frustrate him every day in the beginning.

The language barrier became one of the greatest challenges for Viet and all refugees during their early days in the USA. He remembered that there were nights he would lie in bed crying and wondering how he could truly master the English language and talk like a native person. Some evenings he could not sleep while thinking about the many challenges waiting for him in the new land. Like most refugees, Viet came to this country with only a shirt on his back and nothing else. He had no sponsor or charity group to give him any material or financial help.

He recalled how difficult his first year was in America. He attended school as a senior and took the SAT and the TOFEL to qualify for college during his first semester in the American school system. His English was not good and that made it more difficult for him to understand the test questions. Fortunately, Mathematics, Physics, Chemistry, and Biology use the same symbols throughout the world. So, he guessed what the questions might be about without knowing the author's true intentions. Ironically, he received almost perfect scores for four science subjects. Where he did not do the best was English Composition, Government, and anything that involved the language or knowledge of America. He remembered well the first pop quiz in his Government class for which he did not study or understand thoroughly. He ended up with his first D ever in his life. He was devastated and sad with that result. Back home, he was an all-A student and at the top of his class. This was certainly a great life lesson for him on humility and woke him up to a new reality in his life. That reality demanded that he work harder and figure out what he needed to do with his life.

The language barrier was not the only challenge that a refugee encounters. Like most refugees, Viet left behind most of his family and friends. He had very few family members and friends around him in America. A refugee who already has dealt with an isolated world because of language barrier now face a lonesome one without many friends in the new land. It takes some time to make new friends. In the beginning, a refugee must reach out to his or her own countrymen or faith community to be the source of friendship and support. He or she wants to hang around people who speak the same language and share the same culture. Or, getting together with folks who share the same faith gives a refugee some comfort and reassurance.

Viet recalls how much he looked forward to talking to a Vietnamese in school, at a store, on a street, or at any gathering, especially religious ones. He remembered the first time he saw some Vietnamese kids in school; that moment made him feel like he was connected back to the human family. He asked them for help figuring out where things were in his new school setting. They showed him where he could find certain classrooms, the gym, the counselor's office, or the correct bus.

All that information was very important and helpful to a new student like Viet. He later did take a wrong bus home, and it dropped him off in the wrong neighborhood. He tried to find his way home. Being new to his rental home and first neighborhood in America, he vaguely remembered that his home had a white garage door. Then, he took a quick look around him and realized that many homes had white garage doors. Adding to this lack of exact description of his house or correct address, it was getting dark quickly. He began to get worried and a bit panic that he might not be able to make it home that evening. But, he could not ask anyone for directions with his limited English. All he could do was to come to his faithful and loving God and ask for help in this emergency. His God always came to his aid before and hopefully would bail him out this time. After several minutes of praying and searching anxiously, Viet found his home at last. Another time he had to face a similar emergency, and God came to his aid was when he forgot to ring the bell on the city bus home from school at the right street corner. Because of that mistake, the bus took him all the way to the city bus garage. Again, he prayed for help and God led him home safe after more than a half an hour walk on the street at night.

What Viet learned in the new land was that God was there for him as He had always been since his childhood. If God was not directly involved, He sent His angels such as some caring teachers and kind students to help him. Viet could not believe some concerned teachers and thoughtful students that God sent his way to give him a helping hand at the beginning of his school life. He was grateful to some Vietnamese teachers who used their bilingual knowledge to help him navigate the bureaucracy of the American public school system and get him the right assistance. For example, Viet could not believe how many forms a student had to fill out to be accepted into a public school or how many immunization shots he had to get as a new student. He also appreciated some American teachers who were patient and kind in helping him understand the daily lessons and succeed in their classes. Some students were also considerate and helpful in showing him what to do for some class assignments, while others might hesitate to pick him to be on their teams in a gym class. Viet recalled that many students were often afraid to reach out or take time to explain things for a foreign student. A gym teacher once had to tell Viet which direction to hit the puck in hockey. Apparently, Viet sent the puck back to his goalie whenever he could not go forward with it. In most sports, that was the way to go. However, in hockey one should not do that. Rather, one should dump the puck down toward the opponent's goal and hence give one's team a better chance to score.

But, lacking knowledge of sports and language was not the only reason Viet felt like a leper in the American public school system. Many students were fearful toward a foreign student and even called him names. They would call him, "Jap, go home!" or taunt him, "Let's see some of your Kung Fu moves!" before we saw the social effects of the "Trump" or "Black Lives Matter" movements. Ironically, some African-American kids called him derogatory names the most. Viet certainly experienced the ugly effects of racism and rejection of a refugee personally, long before the world started to address and talk about it regularly.

There are many reasons for someone to have negative bias and ill feelings toward a certain race or a group of people. Sometimes, that happens because a person had a bad experience with someone of a certain background in the past. Or, a person might bully others and decide to treat certain groups badly to show his or her power. Or, someone might be selfish and show no concern for a minority group to display the ugly reality of our dog-eat-dog world. Or, people who show prejudice toward some folks usually act out of ignorance and fear. They do not know a certain culture or custom and decide to shun it or get rid of it out of fear. They feel threatened by the successes or the growth of a certain group of people and want to sabotage that success by treating them badly. Viet was certainly not a stranger to that sort of bad behavior of humanity. He was constantly harassed and name called by the native kids during his first months in America. He ran into all sorts of bad treatment every day simply because he looked different and came from an unfamiliar culture.

However, instead of becoming bitter or feeling depressed and sorry for himself, he was determined to work harder to earn others' respect and concern. He continued to be kind and considerate to everyone, especially his enemies. For he believed in the words of wisdom of St. Paul, who advised all Christians, "Do not repay anyone evil for evil... Do not take revenge, my friends, but leave room for God's wrath, for it is written: 'It is mine to avenge; I will repay,' says the Lord... Do not be overcome by evil, but overcome evil with good." (Romans 12:17-21) Every day Viet tried not to fight with other kids or make waves simply because he had equal rights with his discriminators according to the US Constitution. He wanted to live out his Christian faith and win over his discriminators. He also believed that his faithful God would send the right people to help and defend him. In fact, some African-American teachers were very patient and helpful in guiding him in their classes or pointing him to the right source of assistance in school.

As you can see, a refugee is faced with many challenges in the beginning of his or her life in the new land. One must work much harder than the native and earn everything with sweat and tears. Nothing is given free to a refugee. Viet worked hard on the English language, learned the new culture, faced all the prejudice and bad treatment, tried to cope with personal losses as a refugee, and did everything possible to survive in the new world, even if he had to learn how to eat all the strange foods and get accustomed to the cold weather in the State of Michigan. He spent most of his life eating rice and very little meat. He also enjoyed different kinds of fruits for dessert. But, in the new world, he had to eat lots of meat and very few vegetables at each meal. Desserts also featured very sweet stuff instead of healthy fruit. He usually had to scrape off most of the icing before he could eat a piece of cake or some fancy dessert. One kind of food he found difficult to consume at first was pizza. Most native people might consider it their favorite food, but its tomato sauce made it a bit too strong for his stomach to handle. It took Viet quite a few years before he could train his stomach to retain pizza and learn to enjoy it. Pizza was one of several kinds of foods that he struggled to eat at first in his new land.

In addition to the challenges of the new diet, Viet had to deal with the cold and icy weather. Viet grew up in tropical climate, which is usually hot, muggy, rainy, and wet. Native folks might be accustomed to the cold and snowy weather, but it took a long time for a new resident like Viet to get adjusted to the cold and icy weather in the new world. Furthermore, sometimes weather might affect one's health and make one's daily living completely unbearable for a new-comer. However, there is a hidden blessing in the cold weather: its beautiful snowflakes, which made the cold and icy living in the winter a bit tolerable.

Viet remembers the first time he saw snowflakes in America. It was a quiet morning in his high school senior year, and every student was looking forward to the Thanksgiving break. Suddenly, a student walked up to Viet, tapped him on his shoulder, and said, "Buddy, come over here." Then, he pulled Viet over to a classroom window and pointed to the outside. "Look! See that white stuff coming down now? This must be the first time you've seen snowflakes in America, right?"

Viet was surprised by the question and at the same time mes-merized by the beautiful snowflakes freely floating in the air. He read a lot about winter as a kid and learned to decorate his family Christ-mas manger with cotton for snow. But, he had never seen snow or snowflakes before. This was the first time he had seen snowflakes with his own eyes. His classmates made beautiful snowflakes out of paper and posted them on the classroom windows. Yet, those were not even close in comparison to the real snowflakes and their beauty. Viet could not believe how pretty and proportional the real snowflakes looked as they fluttered freely in the air and floated effortlessly in all directions. It seemed as if they were dancing with the wind and playing a mag-nificent piece of music with nature. The bright sun rays struck some snowflakes and reflected their details to the watchful eyes of many stu-dents in that classroom. Under that beautiful sunlight, the snowflakes looked like little angels floating down from Heaven that landed gen-tly on tree branches and window sills. Viet stood by the window watching those beautiful snowflakes for quite some time without get-ting tired of the splendid show nature presented. He was totally con-sumed by the magical scene of sparkling snowflakes. It eventually led him to think about the amazing God who helped create those snowflakes and bring him safely to the land filled with wonderful things.

His high school senior year was filled with great memories and wonderful learning experiences about life in the new land. It taught him to be humble and open-minded if he wanted to absorb the English language and new culture quickly. It called on him to persevere and work hard if he wanted to survive the long journey ahead. A refugee like Viet had to deal with all sorts of challenges. One of the biggest challenges he had to face in the beginning of living in the Promised Land of America was the lack of resources. He did not have a church or charity organization sponsoring him or giving him any financial or material assistance. All he had was his father, who worked at a minimum wage job making $6 an hour at a local factory. All they could afford was a cheap, two-room rental in the basement of a single home. His jacket was a flimsy windbreaker that he brought over to America from the refugee camp in a tropical country. He could not believe how cold winter turned out to be in the State of Michigan. His father could not afford a warm winter jacket; hence, Viet had to put on a few extra layers of clothing to keep himself warm with his thin windbreaker. But, that made him look bulky and unfashionable to other kids his age on winter days. Yet, he did not mind as long as he could stay warm when went outside in the cold.

His slightly used pair of gloves were donated from a family friend who felt sorry for him upon seeing his bare hands. He did not have any winter boots except a pair of tennis shoes that he had worn for months in the refugee camp. The bottom of those shoes was so worn that it felt like wearing a pair of ice skates in the winter. He used that same pair of tennis shoes in gym class when he was asked to get a special pair for class. His worn tennis shoes were perfect for this setting. He slid all over the smooth gym floor without any problem except when he tried to stop!

Viet did not feel badly that his father could not afford to buy him a new pair of tennis shoes for gym and a good pair of boots for winter. Most native kids were excited about shopping for their school gear and supplies when a new school year is looming. They purchased notebooks, folders, pencils, pens, markers, erasers, glue, scissors, book packs, shoes, clothes, and so on from the stores. Viet did not want to burden his father with the cost of all the school supplies, because he knew his father did not make that much money and had to send money home to Viet Nam to help his family and relatives. He tried to make good use of whatever the school gave him and be creative with the rest of it.

Most people do not know the life struggles that a refugee deals with in a foreign land. Besides the difficult adjustment with the English language, culture, customs, diet, and climate, a refugee has no one to help with daily needs, especially finances. A refugee struggles much more than a native to earn a living and survive one day at a time. But, that earning is not used just for his or her own daily needs. A refugee also has the duty to take care of his or her family and relatives that remain in his or her home country. Although a refugee does not have enough resources, he or she must stretch what he or she earns a lot more and try to help everyone in his or her extended family. Learning how to do more with less is a lifeblood principle for a refugee when dealing with his or her daily challenges.

Viet was proud to spend only $5 for his school supplies at the beginning of the school year: $4 for his backpack and $1 for required folders. He received some free things like used pencils at golf courses, or pens and paper at offices and churches. Imagine if each family spent only $5 per child for each school year. With the additional funds, others could help many disadvantaged kids and charity causes around the world. But, the great principle of "doing more with less" was something that Viet learned back home as a child. Most children in Viet Nam after the war did not have much in their daily life, but they were all pushed to achieve the best results with their school work. Knowing how to read and write and having the basic knowledge of the core curriculum such as Mathematics, Physics, Chemistry, Biology, and a foreign language were required for all high school students. This is why Viet was so surprised to learn that some American kids cannot read or write. He certainly felt badly for them, but he was thankful for the great academic knowledge he had acquired over the years, especially for the opportunity to continue his education in America. Although it had not been easy for a refugee like Viet in America, he appreciated the opportunities that this great country was giving him. He took advantage of opportunities and worked hard to make the best of them. The best part about his story of spending only $5 for his high school senior year was that he achieved high scores on his SAT and TOFEL tests and received a 4.0 grade point average by his graduation day.

The first summer Viet spent in America he looked for work and landed two jobs despite his language difficulties and lack of transportation. He worked at a local factory that produced sports jerseys for forty hours a week, and he sometimes signed up for extra hours of overtime. On the weekend, he had a job at a local restaurant as a cashier or busboy. He averaged about sixty hours a week between the two jobs, both of which paid minimum wage. He used some of that money to help his family here in America and back home in Viet Nam.

Viet slowly built his life in the new land and learn his way around its language and culture. Although he had to take a public bus or ride his bicycle to work, sometimes even in the rain, he did not feel discouraged or sorry for himself. He was grateful for everything God had given him in America and tried to figure out his life's mission that God was calling him to do.

Viet met all sorts of people in school and at work. Some students were kind, caring, and diligent while others were mean, thoughtless, and lazy. He could not believe that many high school students did not take their education seriously. They came to school simply to socialize or be involved in a romantic relationship. They often caused trouble or disrupted the class. Sometimes, they even threatened the teachers with bodily harm or used foul language toward them. Back home, an act like that was not only unthinkable but would bring a student big trouble, including severe punishment. Seeing this attitude in some native students, Viet was determined to work hard and excel academically to make his teachers proud and showcase the great qualities of an Asian student. Some of those qualities are diligence, hard-work, excellence, fast learning, determination, persistence, responsibility, focus, success, and so on. Except for the language barrier, Viet did not think the American high school subjects were that difficult compared to the equivalent required courses in his home country. He also found the whole concept of elective courses in the American educational system quite amazing, because he was required to take certain courses in high school under the Communist education system. There was no choice in anything back home. It took him a while to get accustomed to the American education system of elective courses. This new way of learning lets a student control his or her destiny and choose what he or she wants to learn. Unfortunately, it also sets the bar very low, with many students opting for easy courses to maintain their high grade point averages. However, Viet challenged himself to choose tough courses to make his learning worthwhile.

Viet certainly knew the challenges facing him in the new land. Many of them were beyond his control. The new customs and culture, the strange weather patterns, a new education system, various employment opportunities, and a different governance system were some roadblocks on this great land of America that he had to adjust and maneuver around to survive and succeed in the new world. But, the toughest challenge a refugee faces in a foreign land is loneliness. In some way, it is a battle of will and something he could manage on his own. One must determine ways to control one's mind and spirit and remain sane while dealing with daily challenges. The best way to handle this is to create good relationships either with the divine or with another human being. Many refugees choose to create friendships with both. As a refugee tries to cope with loneliness in a foreign land through friendships, he or she must face the openness of sexuality in Western culture. Everywhere a person looks, he or she finds all kinds of sexual temptations. Viet soon realized that the new land was desperately searching for spiritual guidance and an intimate relationship with the divine. Many of its citizens tried to cry out for a meaningful relationship with the divine based on their search for intimacy and a sexual relationship with another human being. They do not want to feel lonely and become hopeless amidst an impersonal, individualistic, and increasingly challenging world. They wish to belong to a community and have someone like a faithful friend who truly cares about them. Furthermore, they hope their lives have a purpose and that they make a difference in someone else's life. They definitely want to make positive changes in the world and ease others' pains and difficulties. Deep down they all want to be good like their Creator and become productive citizens for their country.

Unfortunately, Americans' lives are surrounded by all sorts of temptations such as lust, money, fame, greed, envy, vengeance, and so on. They struggle to deal with these temptations and try to be good every day, but they fail miserably. They may have a rich and comfortable lifestyle, but their spiritual and mental well-being is neglected. They ignore or put little time and effort into caring for their spiritual life. But, without proper care and nourishment, their spirit and soul will starve, wither, and eventually die. Imagine if someone does not eat and drink or take care of one's body for days. His or her body will weaken, and he or she will soon die. The same thing is true in taking care of one's spirit. A neglected or malnourished spirit and soul causes a person to make wrong judgments and constantly seek out spiritually harmful things.

A spiritually neglected society is fertile ground for all sorts of social problems. Those problems negatively affect the life of an individual and a family over time. As far as Viet was concerned, one's spiritual health encompassed one's mental health and much more. There is no separation between one's spiritual and mental state. It is a big mistake for a society to blame its social problems on mental illness instead of spiritual sickness. It is as if one can separate the mind from the spirit.

Viet recognized the lack of spiritual care in the wealthy and technologically advanced society of America soon after he arrived in the new land. He also saw there were still citizens who were poor, outcast, orphaned, widowed, and lost in America. He was full of the missionary spirit and desire to help others as a newcomer to this country. That spirit and desire was awakened and fostered during the difficult days after the Viet Nam War. His heart was always moved with pity in the face of human suffering and spiritual abandonment.

After much discernment and prayerful consideration of his career options, Viet decided to dedicate his life to become a priest. He felt that by being a priest he would be able to reach out and deal with many of the problems he witnessed in America. Moreover, as a spiritual person, the priestly vocation would help him deepen his love for the Lord and grow his knowledge of the Bible and church traditions. He also felt that it was his responsibility to give thanks to God for saving him from the near-death experience at sea and bringing him safely to the wonderful land of America. His loving and faithful God did not save his life so that he could make lots of money and benefit only himself. Rather, he had been saved and given a new life with plenty of great opportunities for a purpose. That purpose for Viet now was to help others with their spiritual care and share the Good News of God's Son Jesus with the broken world in America. Over time, he hoped he would better understand his life's mission and learn to live his life with joy and purpose.

Viet believed that everyone had been brought into this world for a purpose. God created each human being with a mission. That mission is certainly not to live for one's own selfish reasons, as the first couple discovered in the Garden of Eden. Adam and Eve wanted to be self-glorified and become god themselves by eating the forbidden fruit. They disappointed God and were not sent out into the world to discover their life mission through a difficult life of toil and sweat. God continued to encourage them to discover their life's purpose with the help of the prophets, the saints, and daily revelations. But, they often were caught up in selfish needs and ambitions. Most forgot to figure out their life mission and try to live up to it in their daily life. Many waited until they had a nervous breakdown or their life ran into a crisis before taking time to prioritize it and listen to God's purpose for them. God wanted to help them avoid this problem by offering His Son Jesus on the Cross as the constant reminder to humanity to live for a higher purpose. Jesus' life on earth was short and unflattering. But, it certainly had a noble purpose. His mission was to save the whole world and give it hope to enter eternal life. If each one imitated Him and lived with a purpose, lives would be full of meaning and joy no matter how long or short that life might turn out to be.

A world of people with a noble purpose will surely be peaceful, loving, caring, kind, generous, merciful, thoughtful, and prosperous. Everyone should strive for that noble purpose and allow it to be the guide and driving force of all their actions. They need to reach out to help their fellow human beings and desire to be servants. They should not let wicked desires cause them hurt their neighbors. When everyone learns to follow that way of life, their lives will always be filled with hope and meaning. Nothing in this world, even the dark night of their souls, can make them feel down and keep them from moving forward. Their eyes will be fixed on their God through all the ups and downs of their lives. Their ears will pay attention to the concerns of others and the cries of their neighbors a little more instead of their own needs and benefits. The world will look a little more like Heaven and everyone will behave and become more like angels.

Chapter 12

Searching for God in the Land of Plenty

Viet indeed found his life's mission and desire to serve the Lord and His people in the new land. But, he struggled to find any sign of God's presence in the lives of people he met. There were some churches where he chose to attend after he landed in America. Unfortunately, most of them were not full every Sunday as he accustomed to seeing in churches back in Viet Nam. The only time churches were packed in America was Christmas and Easter. The regular churchgoers call folks who only attend Christmas and Easter Services the "C and E" people. Viet was surprised to discover the low interest in faith in America. Viet was told that interest in faith was worse in Europe, which was the cradle of Christianity, and only elderly people were found in church. Apparently, people did not care about their faith life or have any relationship with the divine in America and other wealthy European nations. They seemed to focus on material possessions and their bodies. They worried about their homes, cars, motorcycles, boats, yachts, clothes, shoes, jewelry, cell phones, electronic gadgets, and other possessions. They spent most of their waking hours protecting and acquiring more possessions. They did that day after day without caring much for their spiritual well-being.

For a refugee like Viet, such a focus did not seem to make much sense. The life of a refugee is one of a nomad. A refugee must leave everything behind and bring very little along. Sometimes, one may have only the shirt on his or her back and nothing else. A refugee must also wander around looking for a job or food to survive. One cannot attach to a lot of material possessions if one needs to be able to move around easily. A lot of possessions make it difficult for one to travel freely and quickly. A refugee tends to lead a simple, detached lifestyle. Although one might not attach to material things, one definitely tries to connect to other people around him or her to find support. Human relationships are more important to a healthy life and the survival of a refugee. Having to leave behind not only one's possessions but also one's relationships, a refugee craves human relationships above all else. Viet recalled how lonely he felt during his first few weeks in America. He did not know the language well and had no friends to talk to. He was confined in a rented room most of the time as if he was in prison. He took every possible chance to connect with others, especially his countrymen.

If a relationship with another human being is so important to a refugee, one can imagine how essential the role of God is in the life of a refugee. God is the only one a refugee can trust and count on. The government or another human being might betray or mislead a refugee, but God will always be there for him or her. God will defend and protect him or her in times of danger. God will comfort and encourage him or her in moments of sadness and doubt. God will give him or her a hand in times of need. God will certainly send the right people to help him or her during his or her early days living in a foreign land.

Viet recalled some of the first friendships he had in America. One of the friends he met in college took him out to an exclusive neighborhood near the school and taught him how to drive a stick shift vehicle. They picked this particular neighborhood because it was quiet and had less traffic, which made the driving practice a little easier. They did not know it was a wealthy neighborhood with tight security. As Viet started up the manual transmission car and let it roll down the smooth, clean pavement with his friend by his side yelling out the driving instructions, everything seemed to go according to plan. Their old, rusty, four-door Chrysler passed by a few homes, and Viet was told to shift to second gear. He tried to pull out the first gear and search for the second gear below it while also pushing in the clutch with his left foot. But, like any beginner, he was clumsy and could not manage all the movements at the same time. The car shook violently and stalled. This embarrassing action happened a few more times. Soon a line of several cars was stacked up behind the Chrysler, and everyone seemed to have a frustrating and angry look. Viet and his friend waved to the drivers behind them to go around the car and let them take time to deal with their stalling problem.

Five minutes later, however, three police cars and three unmarked vehicles rushed Viet's car and blocked it from all sides. They asked him for some papers and then questioned him and his friend regarding why they were there. They questioned the pair a bit more to make sure they did not pose any threat to that neighborhood and then told them to leave immediately. They suggested that they take their driving lesson somewhere else. This was the first time Viet experienced outright discrimination and was treated like a criminal simply because he was in a rich neighborhood. Instead of getting some road assistance, he met the whole SWAT team and was told to go somewhere else. He was told that he did not belong to that neighborhood and was considered a possible threat to its rich members. Apparently, one of the cars behind them called the police on the two Asians and regarded them as a nuisance to their pristine neighborhood instead of giving them some help. After that bad experience, Viet never came back to that neighborhood even though it was near his college campus.

This was an eye-opening experience for Viet about America and its rich history of discrimination. Before setting foot in this land, Viet always thought America was the land of equality, justice, and generosity. That day woke him up to the ugly reality of the way we humans sometimes treat one another. It also showed him how the rich view others around them. They often feel threatened when other people enter their space or encroach on their way of life. They do not think about anyone else except their rich lifestyle and material possessions. On the contrary, Viet was taught to be kind and generous to everyone, even in tough times. He would give anyone the shirt off his back without any hesitation. He would come to the aid of a stranded driver and ask if he or she might need help instead of calling the police. He would invite and welcome anyone to come by his neighborhood instead of kicking out a helpless driver. He would act like the poor widow and her son, who shared their last meal with a stranger like Prophet Elisha, who went by their neighborhood during a drought season and poor harvest (2Kings 4:1-7). A good child of God knows that hospitality and the life of another human being are more important than any earthly possessions and a selfish, comfortable lifestyle.

Viet also learned from the Bible and real life that the poor seem to depend on God more than the rich. They come to God at every chance possible. They put their total trust in God and ask for help often. For they indeed have no one else in the world to defend and help them. They do not have money, power, or fame to fall back on, as do the rich and powerful. Without God, they do not know what to do. God is truly their source of comfort and consolation. God is their strength and hope in dark times. God gives them encouragement and shows them the way to true happiness and peace. God is often their only defender and advocate throughout their lives. The Bible is full of stories about the poor and the lowly coming to God for help. It is very rare that we learn about the rich and powerful coming to God and asking God for anything except maybe forgiveness. The classic story of the poor widow who donated her whole livelihood to the Temple treasury box is one of many examples about the close relationship between the poor and God. The poor widow put her total trust in God and offered everything she had to God's work and ministry (Luke 21:1-4). Her trusting act won high praise from Jesus. She believed that God would take good care of her in good times and in bad. She let God be in control of her life instead of trying to control things on her own. By doing so, God could make the best out of everything the poor widow had. That is the difference between the poor and the rich. The rich typically never allow anyone else except themselves to be in control of their lives. Many think they know everything better than God does. Therefore, they mistakenly cut God out of their daily decisions and eventually their lives.

After the collapse of the Communist country bloc in Eastern Europe in the late 1980s, many of those countries turned to the capitalist system as the new model and stimulus for their ailing economies. Soon their economies turned around, and many were blessed with new-found wealth. Before this miracle, some of these countries were devout Christian countries. Their churches were filled with church-goers every Sunday. People called on God for help for many reasons. Some prayed for daily necessities, while others asked for good health. Some called on God for guidance and help on their decision-making, while others wanted simple blessings and encouragement for their daily lives. Unfortunately, after their lives became a bit more comfortable, they no longer came to God, not even giving thanks for their recent blessings. Churches in Europe these days are quite empty. Churchgoers are mostly elderly. The young, the millennials, and the X-Y-Z generations consider that the idea of God and religion is irrelevant to their lives. They assume that they already have everything figured out, and there is no need for God or religion in their lives. They seek to be in control of their lives and do whatever they feel like doing. They want everything to be fun and entertaining.

But life is full of moments of sorrow and sadness. Our life journey is never a straight and smooth path. We must deal with losses and challenges daily. Our health, jobs, and loved ones can be a source of constant headaches. Sometimes, human resilience and ingenuity are not enough to bring us relief and give us a new life. Only with Divine help can we overcome our daily challenges and live with hope and joy amidst our uncertain world. A believer knows this power well and appreciates it more than a nonbeliever does. Believers do anything to be close to Divine power and receive its full effects. He or she comes to church, makes time daily for prayer, and does whatever it takes to tap into Divine power and use it for his or her daily challenges. Believers know that they cannot make it in life without Divine help. This is the truth, but most people find it difficult to admit. The poor and the lowly understand this truth much better than the rich and powerful. Perhaps this is because poor folks have fewer worldly distractions and can see things more clearly.

Viet lived under Communist rule for more than a decade and grew up with few resources. He might not be allowed to practice his Christian faith freely and had difficult living conditions. But, life back home seemed to be less stressful compared to here in America. He felt that he could find God more easily in Viet Nam than he could in this new land. There were fewer distractions in his home country. Besides, its culture was much more religious and traditional despite the lack of religious freedom. On the contrary, Viet found American culture to be quite secular and materialistic. Furthermore, it was open to various lifestyles and strange ways of thinking. At the same time, this culture has also allowed all sorts of unfathomable crimes and heinous violence to develop over the years. People who carry out such acts of hatred and killing usually do not feel ashamed or remorseful. They tend to feel indifferent about taking the life of another human being and act out of pure hatred. They do not take personal responsibility and honor seriously. They think they can get away without being held accountable for their horrible acts in this life and the next. Worse yet, they might mistakenly assume that God or Allah will reward them for all the pain and suffering that they inflict on other human beings. How can God or Allah praise and encourage evil acts like that? There is no one in his or her right mind that would accept such a belief.

The real God or Allah holds all His creatures accountable for their actions and rewards or punishes them accordingly. Moreover, the real God or Allah encourages us to perform more acts of love and goodness and warns us to avoid acts of hatred and evil. Viet believed that a society that follows God's Commandments and encourages its citizens to search for God's way or noble things instead of human ways or worldly things would experience peace, harmony, happiness, and prosperity. Everyone will know right from wrong and try to help one's neighbors instead of hurting them. Those who think that God and religion are a waste of time must be quite naïve or ignorant about real life and its challenges. Put differently, if a society needs law and order to keep everything moving forward and to avoid chaos, God and religion are certainly needed in the same way for a peaceful and prosperous society. God also helps maintain a person's spiritual wellness and the loving atmosphere of a family. A wise leader of a nation knows how to promote God and religion in his or her society to achieve the best life for his or her citizens, while an ignorant leader will try to suppress or downplay God and religion.

Chapter 13

Searching for Discipline and Routines in the Free Land

Viet surely encountered lots of temptations in the land of freedom to lure him from his calling to follow the Lord and serve his own needs and desires. He was also the oldest and the only son in his family. According to his Oriental tradition, he was supposed to get married and keep his family name going. But, his call to serve the Lord and His Church was so strong that his family let him choose to become a priest against the bewilderment of their countrymen. They questioned his family constantly about how they could allow him to do that and not try to talk him out of it. People thought is parents must be in a lot of anguish to offer their only son to the priesthood, even though they did not show any sign of it on their appearance. Nevertheless, they related well to Abraham and God the Father and saw how painful it was to offer their beloved son for a higher purpose. Imagine if Abraham did not believe in a higher purpose, namely, his faithful God. He would not have obeyed the order of offering his only and beloved son, Isaac, and would have kept that precious gift all to himself. Or, think about this: If God the Father did not see the benefits of working for a higher purpose, namely, achieving human salvation, He would not have offered His only and beloved Son on the Cross and endured that painful loss.

But, anyone who believes in and lives for a higher purpose will usually overcome all the present challenges and be rewarded abundantly in the end. That is exactly what Viet's parents thought and experienced as they let their only son Viet enter the seminary. Still, secular society in America did not make Viet's desire to follow Jesus easy. It made him question his decision to be a priest many times. In the end, however, his life principle of living for a higher purpose, which was the secret that helped him survive all his dark days after the Viet Nam War and as a refugee, won him over and pushed him through the gate of the seminary. What he did not know was that it was just a small hurdle among many big ones that he would encounter in the seminary and later on.

Viet remembered well the day his father dropped him off at the gate of the college seminary. There was little fanfare and no moving trucks. There were only two men—his father and him—and a little hatchback, four-door Chevette. His mother and the rest of his family were still in Viet Nam. Viet had only a small suitcase that held some clothes and a couple of books—an English dictionary and a Bible. After talking to the Rector of the seminary, he and his father bid farewell and parted. The Rector gave him a quick tour of the seminary before showing Viet to his room. The seminary was a two-story, fifty-year-old building that used to be a convent, with a semi-furnished basement. The first floor included the kitchen, dining room, living room, library, chapel, and the Rector's office and bedroom. The second floor featured the seminarians' bedrooms and bathrooms; there was a total of a dozen of rooms, including storage. Viet was given a room at the end near one of the stairways.

Later that day, he met four other men who also joined the priesthood training program that year. They were John, Rick, Paul, and Dennis. John was already ordained a permanent deacon and a bit older than the rest of the group. The Rector called a meeting on Saturday morning to tell everyone about the house rules and program expectations such as morning and evening prayers, daily and Sunday Masses, evening meal together, house cleaning on Saturday morning, dish duty, chapel preparation work, nursing home or God's kitchen volunteering on weekends, and so on. They were also told how to register and take courses at the nearby college, to which they would walk every day. After the long orientation meeting, which was overwhelming to Viet due to the language barrier, they were free to do what they wanted that Saturday evening. Some wanted to go to the local store to pick up some miscellaneous items, and Viet was invited to go along. He could not believe he was able to see the world again after only two days in the seminary. He thought the seminary would keep him behind its walls at least until graduation day. That trip to the store gave Viet some relief and helped bond the group together.

Viet slowly adjusted himself to seminary life while trying to get to know other house members with his limited English. Most foreign students have time to learn the language well before immersing themselves into a full-time college program. But, Viet did not have time and had to learn English and regular college courses simultaneously.

He was also expected to do everything in the house as a regular seminarian even though he only understood a few words out of each sentence.

A funny story Viet recalled about his struggle with the language in the early days goes something like this. Someone might say, "How are you doing?" His mind would take a couple of minutes to process the incoming information along with the speaker's accent. He knew how he wanted to respond. But, there was a delay between his thoughts and what came out of his mouth. By the time he could say, "Fine, thank you," the other person was already long gone. Most of us take for granted our ability to communicate with other people freely and understand everything around us with ease. But, a refugee must struggle with the language among a host of other difficulties in the new land.

All the students in the seminary spent a few hours each day doing their homework, and on some days, they did not have to study for their classes at all. However, Viet would stay up late every night until early morning to do his homework. He had to look up every word on his assignments before he could even read and figure out what they were asking him to do. His desire to learn new vocabulary drove a couple of guys in the house to get him a calendar with a new, long word for each day. He tried to practice words such as "foundling (deserted infant)," "emolument (profit, salary)," "emollient (softening)," "innervate (invigorate)," "insipient (unwise)," "presentiment (premonition)," and so on in daily conversations with people around him. He soon learned that people used those terms in writing, but they do not talk like that in normal conversations. He found himself crying some nights out of frustration and worry about his future in America without a good grasp of the language.

But the language barrier was only part of the tough battle that Viet had to fight in the beginning. He left most of his family and friends back home. He had no support system or anyone to talk to and help nudge him along. He felt alone and overwhelmed by his life burdens. He also worried about the welfare of his father in America and his family in Viet Nam. The thought of hopelessness and suicide did cross his mind. But, he believed he had to keep living for his family and try to carry his heavy cross for his Lord Jesus. Only the desire to live for a higher purpose like that would keep him moving forward with his priesthood training without giving up.

Viet worked hard on his college classes and got involved with all the seminary's activities. Some of those activities taught Viet wonderful lessons about the American lifestyle and culture and left him many sweet memories. Viet recalled the time he was on kitchen duty and had to do dishes after dinner. He put away all the leftovers in the refrigerator and rinsed the dishes before putting them in the dishwasher. Unfortunately, no one told him beforehand that he had to put special dishwashing soap in the dishwasher and not any kind of soap like laundry soap. Viet calmly put the laundry soap in the dishwasher and shut its door thinking that he had done a good job and everything was almost done. All he had to do next was come back an hour later to unload the clean dishes. As he was about to do his homework, one of the seminarians called him down to the kitchen to check out what happened. He could not believe his eyes! The whole kitchen floor was covered with foam and bubbles. It seemed like they came from the dishwasher and kept on coming and coming. The kitchen looked like a bubble show waiting for colorful lights and a performing cast to show up. It took Viet quite a while to clean up that dishwasher mess and put the kitchen back together. That evening, he learned a valuable lesson of the new land: The importance of having the right soap for the dishwasher.

Another incident also involved the college seminary kitchen, when he set off the fire alarm with the microwave. Most people know that one must not put any metal in a microwave, because it can cause fire and an explosion. Despite that danger, there is no clear warning label on a microwave door to remind people not to put anything with even a small trace of metal in it. One day, Viet put a ceramic plate with traces of a metallic decoration on it. As soon as he pushed the START button on the microwave, sparks flew all over the place and his food caught fire. He quickly stopped the microwave and smoke rushed out of the room as he opened the microwave door. The smoke and fire alarms were triggered and sounded their piercing warning about the impending danger. Someone immediately opened the window to clear the smoke, and the smoke and fire alarms gradually stopped. He explained to Viet why the microwave caught fire and what to be put in the microwave in the future. Viet thanked him for that important lesson on how to use a microwave, which was his second in his new life in America.

However, these were not the only life lessons that Viet learned along with his school lessons in the early days of seminary. He learned how to live in a community and get along with others. Over all, there were some fun and memorable moments. But, there were also many challenging and painful moments. One of the fun memories happened when the Rector wanted to challenge a student named Rick to stop smoking. If the Rector won a race, Rick had to turn in all his cigarettes and stop smoking altogether. If the Rector lost the race, Rick would be rewarded with three cartons of cigarettes and could keep smoking happily until his lungs blackened.

The details of the race were not get spelled out clearly, but this was how the two contenders agreed to do. Rector would go down to the basement to get his bicycle and ride it to the nearby college. While doing that, he would give Rick a head start and jog to the college first. Whoever got to the college entrance first would be the winner of the race. The rest of the seminary was assigned a specific task to get the race going and make it a bit celebratory. Viet was chosen to be a referee even though he had never fulfilled this role before or had any preparation. Paul was entrusted with the task of singing the National Anthem. John played the role of the legendary Olympic reporter Bob Costas, while Dennis was the camera man.

On a beautiful sunny Saturday morning in September in the year of the Lord 1988, the highly anticipated race between the Rector and a seminarian took place. Paul helped us kick off the race by singing the National Anthem with his solemn and loud voice, while the rest of us put our right hand on our heart. Everything went well for the first few stanzas of the anthem, but suddenly he stopped and told us he forgot the rest of the words. We were all disappointed that the anthem was cut short and the contenders were forced to start the race a bit early. Without checking to see if both contenders were ready, Viet raised the flag and told them to go. After that false start, he was told to tell them, "Get set. (Pause) Go!" The two contenders took off and the race continued flawlessly, much like a real Olympic race or a Tour de France. The camera kept rolling and the reporter described every move of each contender to his audience. Rick took off immediately and was ahead for the first mile of the race. The Rector descended to the seminary basement to get his bicycle and hurried to catch up with Rick. He quickly closed the gap while the crowd cheering for both.

Unfortunately, after all his years of smoking, Rick did not have much energy and could not pull the last-minute comeback to win the race. The Rector went past Rick, made it to the finish line, and was announced the winner of the race. Rick lost the race and had to stop smoking by turning in three cartons of cigarettes to the Rector. But, stopping a bad habit was never easy. Still, it was a happy time for our group to get together and do something fun. We ate and did a few things like that together for a while. In fact, all five students usually hung out together after Sunday Vespers in the seminary basement to watch the comedy show *Married with Children*. This was one of the ways Viet was introduced to American culture.

However, the happy times for the Rector and his seminarians was soon cut short as the group began to experience infighting. The group fought over many things—from kitchen duty that each had to do to the different viewpoints that they had about various issues. Like any group, they fought and accused each other of all kinds of things. Fights were so intense that they did not talk to each other at the dinner table for the whole semester. The only thing they heard at that meal was the sound of their silverware. Psychologists and counselors were invited to the seminary to mediate conversations and try to relieve some tension among the Rector and five seminarians. Thankfully, Viet did not know much English to get involved with all the fights in the house. He simply did what he was told and focused on his goal of being ordained a priest. But, that did not make it any easier to live with all the tension in the house. The tension became so bad that a couple of members did not know how to handle the annoyances around them and took it out on their neighbors.

There was a neighbor who lived in front of the seminary. This family was loud and constant screaming came from their house. Even their friends behaved the same way. Early every morning, someone came to pick up a member of this household. Instead of coming up to the house and knocking on the door, they honked continuously for a couple of minutes. This loud and annoying act went on every morning. The rest of the neighborhood learned to block it out or ignore it. But, the seminary house members got wound up by all the tension among themselves that one day a couple of them rolled down their windows and yelled out to that anxious driver and neighbors, "Shut up!

Despite that toxic living environment and all the difficulties of being a newcomer to America, Viet was determined and focused on his goal to become a priest. He continued to carry on his duties inside and outside the seminary. He did his duty to bake bread for Mass services as the house sacristan. Although he had done some baking and cooking before, bread baking for use during Mass was not easy. One must get the dough mixture and baking temperature just right if one wants to have good bread in the end. Viet apparently did not follow all the cooking details religiously and decided to cut down his baking time by increasing the temperature a few degrees. Everything seemed to turn out okay with that small change in temperature. But, as soon as the priest broke the blessed bread to distribute to the Mass participants; everything was flying all over the altar. Viet began to feel a little embarrassed by it.

Yet, his embarrassment did not end there. As everyone slowly chewed and consumed the blessed bread, they experienced how hard and chewy it was. Everyone stood and chewed for several minutes, which seemed like forever. Usually regular bread dissolved quickly before a person even needs to chew it. Viet's homemade bread seemed to be hard and chewy. Everyone became impatient after a long period of chewing, and all eyes gradually turned toward Viet as if they wanted to say, "Hey, buddy, what did you make this bread out of? Rock and rubber?" Viet's eyes blinked quickly in response, "Sorry my friends, I messed up on this batch. I promise to do better next time." The problem was that there were still a couple of dozen loaves of this defective bread to be used up yet. The group would have to endure a bit longer until they finished the old batch and could enjoy a new batch of soft, quickly dissolving bread. Viet certainly felt humbled by this memorable experience.

Viet also had to undertake other duties and go through other experiences as part of his priesthood training. His experience with ministries outside the seminary, such as nursing homes and God's kitchen, helped shape his value system and made him a better Christian. Every weekend, he visited nursing homes and God's kitchen to spend time and assist their members. Viet certainly appreciated the opportunities to broaden his life experience and acquire wonderful personal values. For many of his seminarian friends and most Western folks, nursing homes are not their favorite place to visit or discuss.

They are often depressing and sad places. Many families and the public often forget nursing home folks after they had been admitted to these facilities.

Viet was one of the few regular visitors to the local nursing homes and enjoyed his time there. He spent his time doing activities with the residents, chatting with them, and taking them around the facilities in their wheelchairs for sightseeing. With the language barrier, it was difficult for him to understand these elderly at first and vice versa. Over time, they became accustomed to his accent and appreciated his presence more than anything. Viet surely liked to volunteer his time at nursing homes and make friends with these residents. He treasured the stories and life lessons that these wise, elderly folks shared with him. He learned about the values of caring, kindness, compassion, listening, patience, gentleness, honor, and respect. These values helped him relate better to the lives of people around him and made him a caring and compassionate shepherd of God's people.

In addition to the nursing homes, Viet also went to God's kitchen on the weekend to serve the poor and the misfortunate. It was an eye-opening experience for him. He saw people of all ages, backgrounds, races, and genders come through to get a meal. They were mostly individuals, but also families with several young children walked through the door asking for food. Sometimes, children came in right from school on Friday afternoon with their school bags still on their back. Scenes like this brought tears to Viet's eyes. He felt humbled and empathetic toward these young clients of God's kitchen. He tried to mouth "God bless you" to everyone who walked through the serving line as he scooped vegetables or handed them a hotdog. If he did not serve food, Viet helped clean tables and chairs in the dining room or chop onions and prepare food in the kitchen. He often worried about how these poor folks would make it through the week, where they would stay for the night, or what they would do if God's kitchen was not open.

Contrary to that responsible and concerning attitude, Viet often listened to a song sung by Bobby McFarren every weekend on the way to God's kitchen that intoned, "Don't worry! Be happy!" He worried about his challenges in the new land of America and much more, even for all the misfortunate folks at God's kitchen. There was absolutely no way someone could stop worrying. He thought Bobby McFarren was crazy and his song was unrealistic. But, the more Viet listened to the song, the better he understood the message of the songwriter. Bobby McFarren did not say that we could easily stop worrying. Rather, he tried to lift our worrisome spirits and called us to be positive and hopeful in the face of our daily challenges. It was at God's kitchen that Viet met many eager and selfless volunteers who sacrificed their time and effort to serve the lowly and outcast of society. Yet, they did this humble work with joy and love.

One of the volunteers that grabbed Viet's attention was "Mr. Fabulous." He was African American and the cook. Despite his busy work in the kitchen, he was always pleasant and joked around with the volunteers. He gave everyone interesting tasks such as chopping onions and had a good laugh when he saw his helpers crying like a storm after finishing a huge bucket of onions. He would say, "Viet and John, today I want you to help me chop onions." At first, they thought they only had to peel and chop a few and hence joyfully responded, "Aye, aye, Captain!" But, they quickly discovered that we had to work on a huge bucket. It usually meant they would be stuck in the kitchen for a while. That might explain why they cried as their reaction to the scent of onion. Through this experience at God's kitchen, Viet not only learned to be positive and hopeful but also sympathetic, understanding, humble, understanding, sacrificing, and willing to serve. These qualities helped him become a better Christian and a faithful servant leader for God's people.

After a couple of years in the seminary in Michigan, Viet was required to attend his last two years of college seminary outside of the State of Michigan. He had several options for college around the country, but he finally chose one in St. Paul, Minnesota. That meant he would lose all the scholarships and grants from the State of Michigan, which were around $30-$40,000 dollars. Yet, that was not the only challenge Viet had to face. He would be farther away from his family in Michigan and had to attend a new school and a new seminary that would be 20 times bigger than his current ones. Minnesota also had more snow and colder temperatures than Michigan. In fact, he was greeted with a blizzard on his first winter in this new state. There was twelve feet of snow overnight in one winter week, which shut down everything for several days except the pizza and video stores. Viet was mystified that these two stores would be open for students and others to get their fast food and entertainment on snow days, but nothing else sufficed. Abundant snow and bitter cold weather were the first challenges that Viet had to deal with in the new state. The language barrier was still a challenge for him. It usually took him more than double the amount of time than a normal student would need to do his homework and study for a test.

Another challenge, like any refugee in a new land, he had to face was loneliness because he had to move far away from his family and friends. He had to make new friends who encouraged him to do lots of new fun things on the weekends such as dance on Friday evening at the student lounge or watch Saturday Night Live (SNL) every Saturday evening. They thought that Viet studied too hard and needed to enjoy college life a little more. They tried to take Viet out to a local tavern to celebrate his 21st birthday as part of American customs, but this was a bit weird to an Asian immigrant. Most Asian kids had already consumed saki malt since kindergarten as part of Eastern medicine treatment for the annual internal cleansing. Eventually, he met some new friends, and a couple of them invited him to their families' Thanksgiving dinners to avoid a long drive home. He was touched by their generosity and kindness. God surely sent them to Viet like his guardian angels to comfort and lift his spirits in his moments of loneliness.

The biggest challenge Viet faced during his last year of college seminary was the death of his priest, Uncle Fr. Stephen. This uncle had to live in hiding for many years in Viet Nam and snuck out by boat successfully to end up in a refugee camp for a year. He finally came to America and was accepted to serve at a church in Michigan for several months. Viet received the news that Fr. Stephen was involved in a car accident and was killed. Viet's heart sank and his world seemed to cave in when he heard the news. He felt like the Old Testament Job, who apparently lost one family member after another as the result of a bet between the Devil and God (Job 1-42). The Devil bet that Job would turn away from God if his life got tough like losing all his loved ones and possessions. Job went through a period doubting God's love for him and feeling depressed about his misfortunes. Likewise, Viet felt like God had abandoned him. He did not know why God would take away a member of his already small family. Besides, he needed that priest-uncle to be a role model and encouragement for his priesthood training. He was surely in lots of pain and completely devastated. What he did not know was that this painful, difficult event would make him become more compassionate and understanding toward folks who might face the same misfortune down the road. In case he thought he had seen enough death and difficulties in his life, this unexpected tragedy humbled him and could have possibly broken him. Fortunately, Viet used this unfortunate event as an opportunity to make him stronger and ready to deal with whatever life might throw at him.

Adding to this tragedy, Viet had to find a way to get home for the funeral. He could not afford a flight ticket as a full-time student. He lost almost $40,000 of Michigan grants and financial aid by attending college in another state, namely Minnesota, as his Diocese required of him. His Diocese was supposed to pay two-thirds of his tuition as part of its agreement to go to another state for his education. Fortunately, he acquired two-thirds of his tuition in scholarships at his college in Minnesota. That meant his Diocese saved at least one-third of his tuition payment. Viet thought that in a tragic and difficult time like the death of his uncle, his Diocese would step up and help him get an economy ticket for his fight home to attend his family funeral. Despite begging and crying, the leadership of his Diocese refused to help. That meant he might not be able to attend his uncle's funeral. He was utterly surprised and saddened by the cold and indifferent act by the Diocese leadership. He eventually learned that it is the pattern and typical way the Church leadership dealt with lowly folks like him, even though the Lord calls them to love and care for the poor and the misfortunate.

Thankfully, there are many kind and generous people in the world who gladly help unfortunate folks like him. He got in touch with some generous people in St. Paul, Minnesota for help with a flight ticket to Michigan. He was thankful for their kind gift, but also embarrassed that the Diocese for which he studied did not come to his aid in his time of need. Despite the sour taste this experience left him about his Diocese, he tried not to let it make him feel bitter and angry toward the Church and religion. Still, it certainly taught him a great lesson about Church leadership and average people. Church leadership is often cold, indifferent, uncaring, unmerciful, stingy, and stiff. On the contrary, its people are usually warm, kind, caring, compassionate, understanding, generous, and flexible.

This personal tragedy gradually became a thing of the past and Viet graduated with a double major in Mathematics and Philosophy. He was grateful for all the discipline and routines he had acquired from his college seminary years. He did morning and evening prayers, daily Mass, and scheduled activities and meetings of the seminary while keeping up his rigorous academic life. He tried to balance seminary and school, routines and spontaneity, God and friends, and faith and fun. He also had to maintain a part-time job to pay for his books and personal expenses. While many of his seminarian friends had their dioceses, charity groups, and families to help them financially, Viet had no one to assist him. That made him rely on God a lot more and work harder than other students. Amidst a packed schedule of seminary and school requirements, there were two significant activities in which Viet participated during this training period.

The first activity was his year-long internship at a local parish. He experienced the entire Church calendar and its liturgical activities through this internship year. His internship parish had an elementary school—kindergarten to eighth grade. Viet enjoyed visiting students in the classrooms, playing with them on the playground, and going on camping and field trips with them. On one camping trip, he learned how to square dance with the students, collect maple syrup from trees for their pancake breakfast, and make apple cider for the evening's camp fire. The principal saw how much fun Viet had with the students and asked him to create a new sport—soccer—for some of them to play at school. He became their coach, counselor, parent, guide, and friend on and off the field. His players were boys and girls who did not fit in with the popular kids, who tended to be involved in football, basketball, baseball, softball, and cheerleading. He taught the kids about discipline, soccer techniques, teamwork, and most importantly how to lose gracefully. Our life is not about winning at all costs. Rather, a fulfilled life is about knowing how to deal with a loss and move forward without bitterness. Good sportsmanship and conduct was a crucial part of Viet's coaching. He also spent lots of time on the sidelines listening to their problems. This coaching experience helped him learn how to relate well to the children and be a caring counselor for the students.

Also during the parish internship, Viet signed up for prison ministry. This ministry was quite a learning experience for him. He went to prison with a priest to celebrate Mass or went with a lay Catholic to offer a Communion Service every week. Unfortunately, the inmates often would not focus on the service itself, but instead tried to manipulate Viet into shuttling illegal stuff into and out of the prison. Meanwhile, the prison guards appeared cold and mean. Many notorious criminals might look like a normal person, but their rap sheets were awfully long and full of horrible acts. In fact, some of them organized a prison fight, which Viet experienced after just a short time in this ministry. The riot caused a brief prison shutdown—Viet worried that evening that he might not make it out alive. Apparently, the fight was pre-planned and one prisoner tried to attack another during the religious service. Thankfully, no weapon was found, and no one was hurt. Viet also experienced a prison breakout during his parish internship year. Typically, a township tested its emergency siren on the first Monday of the month. One week, the siren went off on Wednesday and made Viet wonder what was going on. Later, he learned on the local news that a prison breakout occurred earlier that day. This incident happened long before the television series "Prison Break" even came out! The inmate could not go far because most of the people who lived around the prison also worked there. He was soon caught and returned to prison.

Another significant activity in which Viet participated during his parish internship was his summer-long work at a hospital in Oxnard, California. This was a memorable experience. Like funeral homes, hospitals are a place people try to avoid. It was certainly not a fun place. People go to the hospital because of sickness, serious wounds, terrible accidents, or an emergency. One of Viet's routines at the hospital was to visit patients and give them spiritual care in the form of prayer and Holy Communion. Sometimes, he was called to the patients' room to listen to their painful stories. A hospital chaplain such as Viet gave patients emotional, mental, and spiritual care, while the hospital staff provided them with physical care. This was the beginning of a holistic healing approach that many hospitals provide a patient today instead of simply putting a bandage on the patient's wound and sending him or her home. Many wounds might have their root in an emotional, mental, or spiritual problem. If the hospital does not address the root of a physical wound, the patient might have to come right back. Viet realized his important role in the hospital's ministry, but did not know what God had in store for him during this time.

Viet's daily routine was to visit patients room by room. He was also assigned to the cardiac floor. Back in the 1990s, heart disease was the number one killer. These days, cancer surpasses heart disease as the main ailment that kills the most people. Viet witnessed traumatic accidents in the Emergency Room (ER), including several triage situations. He met with ER patients' families to deliver important news and comfort them under stressful conditions. Furthermore, a hospital chaplain often shares the saddest news about a person's death with his or her loved ones. Viet found that to be the toughest task that he had to do during his hospital internship. Seeing how devastated people felt upon hearing the difficult news that their loved one did not make it was very difficult for him.

Viet also ran into all kinds of characters during his daily room visits. There were people from different faiths, various backgrounds, and all walks of life. Some warmly welcomed him and wanted to pray or talk with him. Others turned him down and asked for privacy. Some shared with him their personal struggles and issues that weighed them down or bothered them. Those struggles included smoking habits, gambling or pornography addiction, divorce, broken relationships, job loss, and so on. The typical issues that patients often shared with Viet were daily concerns, such as their upcoming surgery, pending tests, mysterious health problems, and sometimes comments about the bland hospital food. Occasionally, he heard some patients talk about their heart-wrenching, dead-end health conditions.

Viet recalled one elderly patient who struggled with death during his hospital internship. She was about 90 years old, but she viewed death worse than a grim reaper. She did not want to die despite her serious illness and having a good life. Viet tried to talk to her to find out the cause of her fears and slowly learned that she was afraid of where she might end up after this life. She did not know where she was heading or what was waiting for her on the other side. That is why she was afraid to let go of her present life and tried to hang on to it. But, a person with a strong faith is typically thankful for his or her life on earth and looks forward to his or her life in Heaven. Earthly life is fragile and temporary, while the Heavenly one is perfect and eternal. After discovering the cause of her fear, Viet set up a plan to bring her peace and tried to help her get in touch with her spiritual life. He surrounded her with prayers and comforting scriptural passages during his visits. She soon found peace in her heart and passed away comfortably within a couple of days.

However, before that happened, she left Viet with a few memorable lines. He remembered visiting her toward the end and seeing her as skin and bones as a nurse tried to give her a shot. Viet could not hide his unpleasant look. She quickly said, "Son, you don't look good!" Viet pointed to the big needle in her skinny arm and responded, "That's why!" He also remembered asking her once about the secrets to living a long and happy life. She answered, "Eat healthy, exercise daily, and avoid bad habits. Also, cherish every moment and try to be kind and caring to people around you." Viet was certainly grateful for that advice.

Hospitals are usually the place where people find healing for their physical wounds. But, Viet learned through his hospital internship that emotional and spiritual wounds can sometimes arise in that setting as well. People usually think that their wounds and sickness will be cured at the hospital. They tend to be confident and place great trust in the hospital. As such, some people want to share with the hospital chaplain and staff other problems that might have affected their health and well-being. Furthermore, having quiet, free time in the hospital setting helps a person reflect more deeply on various issues that might be bothering him or her and try to resolve those issues. Certainly, a patient has plenty of time in the hospital to think about his or her mortality and most want to make peace with everyone.

Viet remembered more than a dozen patients during his hospital internship that talked with him about their emotional and spiritual problems. Some told him their church problems and why they have not been to church. Others shared with him their family and relationship problems.

He remembered a middle-aged woman sharing information about her painful divorce and her broken relationship with her daughter. She had been divorced for some time, but that wound was still tender, just as if the divorce happened yesterday. She had a tough time forgiving her ex-husband and forgetting all the hurtful things he did to her. First, he cheated on her and lied to her about it. Then, he abused her verbally, emotionally, and physically, especially when he was inebriated. Finally, he took all the family's money and ran out on her, leaving her with three young children. Listening to her story brought tears to Viet's eyes. He did not blame her for being angry at her ex-husband and having a tough time letting go of that painful memory. What caught his curiosity was how she overcame that setback and raised a young family on her own. Who gave her strength and hope during those tough and dark nights of her soul? How could she find purpose for her life and move forward each day?

Certainly, it was not easy in the beginning. She told Viet she had few resources and had to live paycheck to paycheck. She worked two jobs while raising her young family. There were times she wanted to give in and end her life. Thankfully, she developed her faith and received divine grace from above to keep her going. She thought about her young family, which would not have a mother to look after it. She imagined the lingering pain and all the questions her loved ones would have if she suddenly departed. Worst of all, she could not imagine looking at her Lord Jesus at the Gate of Heaven after what she did to get there.

So, she thought over that wicked intention and decided to use her life for a higher purpose. That purpose for her was to raise her young family in the love of God. After she set her sights on that purpose, she felt a lot better. She overcame her fear and replaced it with hope and courage. She found strength and determination to take good care of her young family. God also gave her a hand with the tough tasks she faced by sending the right people her way to help her out. She certainly was stronger and much more confident now than the day she was left to fend for herself. But, she still found it extremely difficult to forgive what her ex-husband did to her and her young family. Perhaps with time and God's grace, she would be able to forgive him and leave that painful past totally behind.

Viet left the hospital that summer to go back to school with a grateful heart and a much more caring attitude. He learned a lot during those three months at the internship hospital about spiritual care, especially human emotions and spirit. Still, he signed up for more years of graduate school to get his Master of Divinity Degree. That schooling in Chicago, Illinois helped him pick up significant academic knowledge about Theology, Scripture, Sacraments, Church History and Tradition, Moral Ethics, Canon Laws, and so on.

During this school period, Viet heard about an alleged improper relationship between a male seminarian and a priest staff member. All sorts of media scrutiny surrounded the incident, especially after news exploded regarding child sexual abuse by clergy and the Church cover-up. Along with this story, his seminary was accused of allowing a homosexual culture and practices among its priests and seminarians. Perhaps the Church might ease up its standards and allow gay seminarians to be ordained someday. However, Viet saw no evidence of a homosexual culture in the seminary during his years there as was reported. If there was any homosexual activity occurring at his school, it must have been done secretly.

The solid majority of the seminarians were heterosexual, and everyone was expected to treat one another with respect and compassion regardless of sexual orientation. A person's sexual orientation was simply a private matter, and no one cared to find out about it. The seminary had its tough standards to screen out and evaluate its candidates at the beginning and throughout the training process. A seminarian would be evaluated by his seminary board, dormitory priest, and peers. His peers might rate him with a neutral answer; that alone might cause him serious scrutiny by the seminary staff. The seminary might somehow ordain a homosexual priest, but its standards were always tougher than nails.

Looking back on those graduate years of seminary, the best memories for Viet were two pastoral experiences for which he signed up. The first experience was the Appalachian trip. Viet and a dozen of his seminarian friends voluntarily drove down to the Appalachian region one morning and spent a week helping build homes for local folks. It was a humbling and memorable experience. As an immigrant, Viet could not believe part of the country like Appalachia existed within the wealthy America. The contrast was stunning and heartbreaking. Viet and his friends helped frame the house, put up insulation and rock sheets, ran electrical wires, laid tiles and a wood floor, painted, installed doors and windows, and achieved some other miscellaneous things. They completed significant work, but also had lots of fun helping some of the poor folks in our blessed America.

They also had time off to see some local scenery and enjoy the beautiful nature of the Appalachian region. Viet was touched by the friendly, easy-going attitude of the local folks and their distinct accent.

The week soon ended, and they had to return to the seminary. But, Viet would never forget that humbling and eye-opening experience of serving others in America. Politicians, with their divisive rhetoric, often blame the country's problems on foreigners and accuse immigrants of taking all the country's resources but contributing nothing to society. Most reasonable people know that is not true. Immigrants like Viet might need help in the beginning, but they will return that favor and give back to society a hundredfold once they are established. Viet found it to be a blessing and humbling experience for him as an immigrant to help the natives in America with his house-building work on the Appalachian trip.

Another memorable experience he had during his years of graduate school was his trip to El Paso, Texas to help immigrants on both sides of the US–Mexico border. Viet drove south to El Paso with a dozen seminarians from Chicago in a van using the traditional map to navigate. Unfortunately, the navigator rolled down the van window for some fresh air and the wind pulled the map right out of his hands! Keep in mind that there was no Global Positioning System (GPS), MapQuest, or Google in the 1990s. Thankfully, Viet's group managed to get to their destination safely after some prayers and help from some gas stations.

The group stayed in a local home where immigrants were given food, clothing, and other necessities. They were also warned that Immigration and Naturalization Service (INS) agents could storm the home and raid the neighborhood in the middle of the night. On the way to this home, they went through numerous checkpoints and roadblocks. It felt as if they were in the Middle East or a war zone. For Viet, everything here brought back painful memories of the Viet Nam War and its horrific end. Checkpoints and roadblocks were a common scene and part of daily life for Viet during the war. The night raids were another remnant of the war as the Communist government routinely searched homes and took attendance of the residents without legal authorization.

Thankfully, there were no night raids during Viet's stay in El Paso. They shared a couple of simple daily meals with the immigrants and listened to their difficult journeys to America. They came from various countries in South America: Guatemala, El Salvador, Bolivia, Columbia, Mexico, and so on. They were grateful to come to America in one piece, but nervous about the INS and their ability to stay in the country. They constantly stayed alert and kept to themselves most of the time.

After staying on the US side of the border for several days, Viet's group went with the guide to cross the border and enter Mexico. They came to a little town near Juarez and spent the night there. They saw this same town across the border the night before under the starry sky. It was lit up, but its light was a bit more yellow than the one on the US side. Now, they saw it in person. Most of its homes were makeshift shacks and some were even made of cardboard. The roads in town were all dirt and quite narrow. Close-up, this little town looked like a refugee camp, and Viet spotted an interesting feature. Some of the homes were built of cardboard, but some had a huge satellite dish next to them. Clothes lines and containers to catch rain were seen all over town. Water trucks drove through the town once a day to bring residents the precious commodity in this desert-like region. Because water was the rare commodity, Viet and his friends were given only a small glass of it every morning to brush their teeth and wash. However, they were advised not to drink it, because they could possibly become sick from it. Instead, they drank Coke or bottled water. It was not a pleasant stay, but that was how they learned to empathize with the plight of the lowly and outcast of society.

They also visited several US companies in Mexico to see how workers were paid and treated compared to their American counterparts. For a few free hours of the day, they checked out the outdoor market in Juarez for some gift and souvenir shopping, but were cautioned to stick together and be safe due to the notorious local drug gangs. Juarez was known for drug dealing, kidnapping, hostage ransom, and violent killings by rival drug gangs. Thankfully, they all came home safely and stayed in Mexico for a second night before heading back to the US.

The north-bound border crossing was a bit tougher than southbound as they were thoroughly checked for a long time. Viet was grateful and happy to be back safely in the US. He was humbled to experience the plight of an immigrant from South America and the desert life along the US-Mexico border. Most normal Americans do not know how these poor, forgotten people live day by day. Only by getting out of their comfort zone and putting themselves in others' shoes were they able to develop compassion and learn to treat one another kindly, just as they wanted others to do for them (The Golden Rule).

Although an immigrant along the US–Mexico border faced challenges every day, Viet could speak from personal experience how much more painful and difficult it was to get to America for an immigrant coming from a Communist country. Viet had no freedom or rights, whereas many South American immigrants have limited rights in their home countries. And, the definition of poverty in the Western world is different than that where Viet came from. A poor person in Viet Nam means that he or she does not have anything at all and has to beg for food every day. Although some were living in cardboard houses, anyone with a satellite dish must be rich. Finally, Viet had to pick up a completely new language and set of customs compared to South American immigrants. Despite these differences, Viet sympathized with their plight and challenges as newcomers in America.

Chapter 14

Searching for Human Care in the Church,
the World, and Daily Life

Viet was thankful for the routines and discipline he picked up in the seminary. After ten years of seminary training, he was ordained and sent to his first parish assignment. He brought along all the training, advice, academic knowledge, routines, discipline, and prayers to his first church and future churches. He felt confident and could not wait to pass on his knowledge of the spiritual life to God's people. He was a bit idealistic and thought he could conquer the world. What he did not realize was that his theoretical world would clash with the real one and that experience would help him acquire new knowledge about the Church in the modern world.

Although the percentage of church goers is still higher in America than in Europe—the birthplace of Christianity—that number has been decreasing steadily over the years. Most churchgoers today are elderly and white-haired or no-hair folks. The young do not find church and religion relevant to them. It is difficult to find a young family to be regular churchgoers. But, interest and relevancy is not the only problem that the Church faces in the modern world. It continues to get tangled in all sorts of social issues that create division and civil war among its members. It gets divided into thousands of small groups with their own missions, and these groups often do not collaborate and work with each other for the sake of their Lord Jesus. Compromise is not a word they want to hear. They would prefer everyone else to rally around their point of view and follow their ways.

What saddened Viet as a young priest about this division and infighting within the Church was that it reminded him of the Church's past mistakes and played right into the hands of the Prince of Darkness. Viet knew about stories of division and infighting in the Bible and how each ended. A couple of well-known ones are the war between the houses of David and Saul (2Samuel 2:8-4:12) and King

David's family feud (2Samuel 15:1-19:8). King Saul became jealous of David and his support from the people and wanted to destroy him. This infighting caused hurt and division within the kingdom. Meanwhile, King David's son, Absolon, and his allies decided to stage a coup against his father. His act of division brought about turmoil, chaos, pain, anguish, hurt, killing, and civil war in the kingdom. It affected the well-being and growth of the kingdom for quite some time.

The Church also went through infighting and schisms over all kinds of issues. These fights divided the Church East from West, pitched Protestants against Catholics, and moved the papacy from Rome (Italy) to Avignon (France). They not only brought about pain and bloodshed but also caused the Church to lose resources and effort. Like many mistakes in the Bible, Viet saw that God's people kept repeating the same mistake one generation after another and wondered if they would ever learn. The sad part is that they have not learned anything at all.

We have seen this problem throughout the Bible and Church tradition. God's people repeated the same mistakes in the Bible by making wrong alliances with foreign powers and paying a heavy price for it when that power collapsed. Similarly, the Church leadership did not let humility and compassion guide its policy decisions; this mistake caused all kinds of problems for its people. It carried out its controversial policy of converting non-Christians by threatening him or her with the sword. That policy is often called the Inquisition. Because of the dark and evil history of the Inquisition, Christians today still get blamed for this mistaken policy.

Another mistake the Church made that led to infighting and schisms was its involvement with power, possessions, and pride. Church leadership was more concerned about these things instead of peace, harmony, unity, humility, compromise, and reconciliation. This is why the Church has been divided into thousands of factions since Jesus' time. Over the centuries, many good folks have tried to unite the Church and mend the wounds of division. They have produced some success, but left many unresolved divisions in the Church. Worse yet, the Church has engaged in more divisive, controversial issues than working on uniting, common issues over the years.

Nothing good ever comes out from division, faction, schism, and infighting. This is exactly what the Prince of Darkness wants the Church to do. This is exactly his game plan. Unfortunately, the Church is too blind to see it. The Church could not figure out the Devil's game plan or do a regular self-examination to determine if its agenda and issues were leading it away from Jesus or not. Jesus apparently left great advice over the issue of division and infighting. He said, "...Every Kingdom divided against itself will be ruined, and every city or household divided against itself will not stand. If Satan drives out Satan, he is divided against himself. How then can his kingdom stand" (Matthew 12:25-26)? Paul concurs with Jesus and adds this, "... I urge you, brothers and sisters, to watch out for those who cause divisions and put obstacles in your way that are contrary to the teaching you have learned. Keep away from them. For such people are not serving our Lord Jesus Christ, but their own appetites" (Romans 16:17-18). Neither Jesus nor Paul saw anything good in division or infighting. Unfortunately, the Church, especially its leadership, could not see the harm and destructive power that division and infighting caused its members. It should find ways that help it avoid these harms and promote more unity, peace, harmony, compromise, and reconciliation.

The best test of good leadership is someone who can provide these qualities. Any leader who creates division and infighting is not a good one. Instead, a good leader does anything in his or her power to maintain and promote unity, peace, harmony, compromise, and reconciliation. Again, Jesus left with us a great example on testing good leadership as He asked Peter a series of questions. "When they had finished eating, Jesus said to Simon Peter, 'Simon, son of John, do you truly love me more than these?' 'Yes, Lord,' he said, 'You know that I love you.' Jesus said, 'Feed my lambs.' Again, Jesus said, 'Simon, son of John, do you truly love me?' He answered, 'Yes, Lord, you know that I love you.' Jesus said, 'Take care of my sheep.' The third time He said to him, 'Simon, son of John, do you love me?' Peter was hurt because Jesus asked him the third time, 'Do you love me?' He said, 'Lord, you know all things; you know that I love you.' Jesus said, 'Feed my sheep'" (John 21:15-17). Jesus wanted a leader like Peter, or anyone who claims to love the Lord, to serve God's people and take good care of them—adults and children alike.

Unfortunately, most leaders do not share the same thinking with Jesus and tend to focus on themselves and their personal glory and agenda. That is why all sorts of contradictory viewpoints, division, and infighting occurs in the Church. Viet saw very little care and compassion being shown among Christians, especially from Church leadership. There was a lot of judging and condemnation in the Church, even though that role should be reserved solely for the Lord on the Last Day. This infighting and chaos plays into the hand of the Prince of Darkness and is exactly what he wants. Church factions have been too busy fighting each other to recognize the emerging threats caused by the power of darkness. Violence, killing, and lack of concern for the gift of life have become the common theme of daily news headlines. Viet believed that all Christian factions should make peace with one another and focus their fight on the power of darkness and nothing else. They should go a step further and collaborate with other religions to fight evil and hateful ideologies to promote peace, harmony, compromise, reconciliation, and love. That is the world all people of good will should work for and promote.

Viet will always carry with him the scars of the Viet Nam War. His people still pay a high price for many more generations because of that war. He is sad that South Viet Nam and the US lost the war to North Viet Nam and the Communists. But, he is thankful that the painful war ended despite the enormous sacrifices that many South Vietnamese like him have had to make. Some lost their lives, while others have been forced into exile and face the life of a refugee. Many more continue to suffer in Viet Nam under the control of the oppressive Communist regime. But, at least Viet Nam is now at peace. There is no more bloodshed, killing, or violence. People live in stable conditions under the watchful eyes of the Communists. That is an expensive price that Viet and all the Vietnamese have paid for a life of peace.

Christians and the Church must consider paying the same price and making great sacrifices if they want peace and harmony in their daily lives. Otherwise, constant fighting and various factions will continually plague the Church. Every Christian must make personal sacrifices if peace, harmony, compromise, reconciliation, unity, care, compassion, and other wonderful virtues are to take root and be a part of the Church life.

And yet, infighting and factions are not the only problem that the Church has faced over the years. Another problem Viet has seen is waste of resources and lack of accountability. Coming from a country where resources were scarce after the war and having to survive as a refugee with only the shirt on his back, Viet could not believe how wasteful the Church was with its resources and donations. He can see this wasteful problem at the government level because of its lack of accountability. But, he was shocked to see how much money was spent on pompous and fancy things, while many folks struggle to find food each day around the world. Many people in the Church have not had to endure a day without a morsel of food and do not understood the pain and worry that the poor face each day. Viet had been through days without food after the war and lived through time in prison under the Communist system with very little food. He understood the daily struggle of the poor for food quite well. He never wanted to throw out any expired food and had to ask his parish housekeeper not to empty his refrigerator just because something was a few days old. He tried not to waste any food and ate everything people put in front of him. That is why his friends in the seminary nicknamed him the "The Little Garbage Disposal."

Viet is glad that Pope Francis has addressed the issue of wastefulness in the Church and called on his Church and the world to cut down unnecessary use of resources. The Pope has tried to cut down on spending at the Vatican and other Church celebrations. He wants each Christian to be a responsible steward of the resources with which his or her Creator has entrusted him or her. That surely pleases our Lord Jesus, who evidently shared several parables about good stewardship and the Kingdom of Heaven. Viet believes that by reducing our tendency to waste resources, Christians will follow our Lord's teaching and hold ourselves accountable to our Creator. Stopping waste is a way for us to be green and be a good steward of the planet. Along with cutting waste, the Church could learn from businesses to spot talent and foster gifted people to advance the mission of Jesus and help draw the world closer to the Kingdom of Heaven. Failing to be a good steward and promote the right talent will surely disappoint the Lord on the Last Day.

Like any organization, the Church has a problem with accountability. It has a problem holding people, especially people in leadership, accountable for their actions. Like the real world, powerful and rich folks can get away with anything in the Church. They use their power and money to buy favors and influence in the Church any way they want. Viet thought the Church faced this demon in the Reformation as Luther pointed out in his 95 Theses and denounced it for good. Unfortunately, power and money continues to influence the Church negatively, just as it does in our country's politics. Powerful and rich folks threaten to reduce their church donations if they do not get their way.

Being idealistic and naïve to his calling of serving the Lord and His people, Viet has never taken that threat seriously. He has often told these folks that he is grateful for their donations to the Church, but he would not let them use power and money to influence him. Besides, he has faced poverty since childhood and survived under harsh living conditions. He has courageously stood up against the rich and powerful throughout his ministry. Once, Viet tried to hold some folks who were on the School Board accountable and make them conform to its by-laws and good Church stewardship. But, his efforts went nowhere as they kept violating the by-laws and doing things their own way without caring about wasting Church resources. They did not look out for the welfare of the whole school and the Church and address tough issues such as low enrollments, marketing, or the proper way to discipline a misbehaving student. They even chastised board members or parents who did not follow their ways in the board meetings. The only option left for Viet was to clean house and let them all go.

Unfortunately, Viet did not get support from the higher authorities. He further learned that the Church authorities listened to the rich and powerful and would not give him the benefit of the doubt and back him up. He was saddened and disillusioned that an institution to which he had dedicated his whole life would betray and abandon him in the face of wealth and power. However, this was not the first time Viet was mistreated. It happened before. Along with this mistreatment, he felt discriminated against in his Church. He witnessed how a white priest was treated compared to a minority priest like him. He saw how some priests wrote and described their priestly ministry like a wonderful walk in the park. These priests were too naïve or disingenuous about the challenges of following the Lord and serving His people in a Church that is badly divided and negatively influenced by money and power. It is tough to be a priest in the 21st century, especially if one is a minority. If it were not for his love and commitment to the Lord and encouragement from his family and friends, Viet would not have had the strength to continue his priestly ministry. He would have walked away from the ministry and found other ways to serve Jesus and His Church. But, it was the love of Jesus that gave him purpose and hope to keep his ministry alive. He was certainly heartbroken by the treatment of the Church leadership and some wealthy Church members toward him.

But, what troubled Viet the most is the lack of care and compassion in the world these days. People's hearts are filled with anger and hatred. They act out of that dark and bitter emotion and hurt many innocent people around them without regret. They use violence and killing to express their emotions and points of view. Viet wondered, "Can we learn to live in peace and make compromises with one another? Can we try to show care, compassion, love, and respect toward one another before any ideologies?" Viet believed that when we humans can swallow our pride and learn to show God's love to one another, we can see God's presence a lot easier. The way everyone treats one another right now, God seems so far away from our world.

Despite some challenges in his priestly ministry, Viet had many sweet memories surrounding the Sacraments. He remembered fondly the first babies that he was honored to baptize as a deacon. The whole baptismal ceremony takes about half an hour with all its rituals. However, half an hour is a long time for little kids to stay still and keep quiet. Noon is also a time for kids to eat and take a nap. Viet did not know kids' whole schedule. So, he conducted the baptism as normal and went on with its lengthy prayers. Suddenly, one baby started to cry. Then, another one joined in. Soon, all seven babies were screaming at the top of their lungs, and the congregation "enjoyed" a whole concert sponsored by babies. Viet became so nervous that he skipped two holy oils (Oil of Catechumen and Sacred Chrism) and jumped right to baptizing them with Holy Water before chaos broke out. Slowly the babies started to quiet down and Viet recalled that he forgot the anointing part of the two oils. He quickly went back to anoint them with the two holy oils.

Reconciliation or Confession is usually a time for tears and sobbing as a penitent tries to turn his or her life around. But, Viet had some chuckles when looking back on this Sacrament. Once, he worked on a few church projects and had to rush into the Confessional room without any rest. He decided to grab some quick shuteye. He does not know how long he sat in the room with his eyes closed. Suddenly, he opened his eyes and saw a little kid sitting right in front of him saying nothing. He was a bit embarrassed and asked the child on how long he had been sitting there. The kid did not say anything. Viet suspected that he probably went home and told his parents about a sleepy priest in Confession. A lot of folks would love to go to Confession with a sleepy priest to get easy penance!

Another funny story involved with this Sacrament for Viet happened when he did Confession with another priest for a large group of students. Several parents came to him the day after and asked him why the other priest only let their kids confess just one sin. It must be confusing and nerve-racking for a penitent trying to figure out which sin was worse to confess. Except for the notion of saving time, there is no Confession rule that tells someone to confess only one sin. A penitent can confess as many sins as he or she wants. That priest must have run out of penance to give for anything more than one sin!

Finally, many older folks were taught to go to Confession first before they were worthy of receiving Holy Communion. Viet was asked to visit an elderly man at a nursing home and let him go to Confession so that he could receive Holy Communion. Viet came to the gentleman's room dressed like a lay person and asked if he would like to receive Communion. The elderly man did not recognize Viet as a priest and hence told him that he needed to go to Confession before he could receive Communion. Viet finally told him that he was a priest and would be glad to hear his Confession. The elderly man now had no more excuse for not receiving Communion and had to tell the truth that he did not want to take Communion or do Confession for that matter. So, he told Viet that he needed a Bishop to go to Confession. Viet could not hold back his laughter and told the man that he would try to contact the Pope so that he could go to Confession. Then, he thanked the elderly man for his time before departing.

People often think Mass or the celebration of the Holy Eucharist is boring and routine. The truth is that one does not know what might happen from one Mass to the next. Some child, for example, might scream at the top of his or her lungs. Or, an Altar Server might pass out from being overheated. Viet remembered at his first parish assignment there was an early Mass at 7:30 am on Sunday. It was rare to find a child at this Mass, and it was usually poorly attended because of its early time. Once, Viet was blessed to have a kid as his Altar Server. Everything went well until everyone sat down for the Scripture readings. After the first reading, some folks in the front rows started to whisper and focus on the Altar Server. Viet turned to his left and saw the Server slowly leaning to the side and then falling to the ground. Thankfully, he did not hit his head on the marble floor. He quickly got up, dusted off his embarrassment, and went right back to sleep in his chair. Viet could not believe what he was seeing and wanted to ask the boy if he was all right. Now, however, Viet was afraid that he might wake him up with his questioning! Viet was pretty sure that the boy slept through the homily at that Mass as well.

Like that boy, Viet found early morning Mass could be a challenge for him sometimes. He remembered that once he tried to lead the congregation in an opening song with a familiar tune. Everything seemed to go well until they came to the end of the song, and they found themselves running out of words to accompany the tune. That was when Viet learned that he used the wrong tune and had to end the song abruptly by saying, "People, I think that is enough singing for today!"

Another fun memory that Viet had about Mass was that one of his participants passed out during his homily. People often fall asleep during homily time because the topic or the homilist is not interesting. But, Viet never saw anyone completely passed out in church before. Apparently, this person had a small stroke or a mild heart attack, and the whole EMS crew came in the middle of the Mass to perform CPR. Viet had to pause the Mass and give him Last Rites. Later, some of Viet's friends joked with him that it must be his "fire and brimstone" homily that caused the man to have a stroke or heart attack. The elderly man was taken to the local hospital and recovered nicely after that.

One more sweet memory about the Mass happened when Viet helped at a church when its pastor was on vacation. It was a tradition of this church to make a big loaf of bread to re-create what took place at the Last Supper. But, the Church did not know how many people planned to attend each Mass so that it could determine the number of loaves needed. It decided to have one loaf and use small wafers to make up the rest. The loaf was broken into small pieces and mixed with all the wafers at Communion time. Everyone was handed a small piece of consecrated bread or a blessed wafer depending on the luck of the pick by the Communion minister. Everyone was fine with whatever the minister handed him or her. After all, it is the Body of the Lord Jesus. Suddenly, a little boy showed up in Viet's Communion line. Viet randomly picked from his ciborium a small piece of consecrated bread and handed to the boy. Instead of giving the expected answer—"Amen"—the boy loudly said to Viet, "Can I have the chip?" Viet's jaw dropped when he heard it and did not know what the boy meant. Suddenly, it hit him that the boy was referring to the blessed wafer. Viet was about to say, "Wrong answer!" but he held back and gave the boy a blessed wafer without saying anything to him. It was certainly an eye-opening experience for Viet to see how God's people view the Holy Eucharist.

As we talk about the Holy Eucharist, Holy Thursday is a special day, because Jesus left with us this great Sacrament at the Last Supper with His apostles. Also, on this special evening, He did the most loving and humble act for them by washing their feet and asked them to do the same for one another. Viet recalled at one of his parish assignments, twelve chairs were set up at the foot of the sanctuary area for this solemn ritual as expected. Unfortunately, there was a miscommunication and a thirteenth person showed up. Viet tried to tell this young man that there were already twelve people and thanked him for showing up. But, he refused to leave. He sat down on the Sanctuary step and began to take off his shoes and socks. The congregation had never seen thirteen people have their feet washed and started to laugh awkwardly. To help break the tension, Viet made a comment, "I guess Matthias showed up a bit early to replace Judas, heh?" (Matthias was chosen by the eleven apostles to replace Judas.) This funny incident reminds Viet to stay alert always because interesting things can happen at any time during a Mass.

Some people might think that the Confirmation ceremony is usually long and boring. This ceremony is typically reserved for the Bishop unless he delegates it to a priest. Interestingly, Viet served as the Bishop for a day. It happened that his Bishop suddenly passed away a couple of days before he was scheduled to come to Viet's parish for Confirmation. There was no spare Bishop who could come to the church on such a short notice for that special ceremony with the youth. So, Viet was delegated to perform Confirmation for that special group of youths and forced to be the Bishop that evening. The whole congregation held its breath in anticipation of how Viet might handle this unusual and special event. Suddenly, they saw him put on a Cheese hat, which was a gift from a die-hard Green Bay Packers fan and hold high a beautiful walking stick, which was given to Viet by a veteran friend. The tension before the ceremony quickly disappeared, and everyone burst out laughing. Viet told them that was as close to being a bishop as he could get. The whole Confirmation ceremony went without a glitch. After the ceremony, every Confirmation candidate and many attendees came up to Viet and asked for a picture with him, the Cheese hat, and the walking stick.

Another joyful Sacrament that left Viet with fun memories was the Matrimony or Wedding. He has seen missing grooms, fainting bridesmaids, crying flower boys and girls, and so on. However, for one unforgettable wedding, Viet was honored to preside for a young couple. The whole wedding went well as planned in the beginning. Then, the mothers of the couple were invited to come up and light the family candles on both sides of the Unity candle to symbolize the couple's birth families. After the Scriptural readings and the exchange of the marriage vows and rings, the couple lit their Unity candle from their birth family candles. The cantor was singing and the congregation joined in with gusto. Suddenly, the fancy ribbons around the candles caught fire and the entire Sanctuary was quickly filled with smoke. This newly wedded couple literally sparked a new flame with their love! Ironically, no one in the congregation moved out of the pews to open a door, nor did anyone try to put out the fire. Meanwhile, the cantor did not see the thick cloud of smoke in the sanctuary or smell the burning ribbons. She kept on singing without missing a note. Viet could not let the charade go on any longer and rushed to the untamed fire to put it out. He thought about asking people to clear out of the church for fear of smoke inhalation. But, he figured that a little holy smoke would not hurt, and the wedding ceremony continued. However, he did try to open a couple of side doors to vent the church a little. Thankfully, this wedding ended peacefully without any further incident.

A priest often must switch gears quickly and go from joyful events like a wedding to somber ones like hospice and funerals. Viet got calls to visit hospitals, nursing homes, hospice facilities, and residents to give the sick and the dying the Sacrament of Anointing or the Last Rite. Whenever people hear the phrase "Last Rite," they are usually freaked out and try to delay this ritual as long as possible. Viet remembered one day he walked down a long hallway of a Home for Veterans, where he had served as its chaplain, to visit a dying veteran. He was all dressed up for this important visit. A member stopped him and asked, "Hi, Father! You look nice and very formal today. What is going on?" Viet responded, "Hello, Dave! I was called to visit a member who is really sick and perhaps give him the Last Rite." Dave paused and answered, "Well, in that case, stay the heck away from me! I don't need the Last Rite yet!"

Viet saw this reaction a lot regarding this Sacrament. No one wants to hear about death and dying. But the truth is that Viet saw how this Sacrament worked miracles on the sick. Some of them, after being anointed, recovered and got well. Others found peace and passed to the next life without much anguish. The faithful also called him before surgeries for this important Sacrament to make peace with the Lord and ask for healing grace and extra help from above. There were times Viet had to run alongside the gurney to administer this Sacrament of Anointing as the nursing staff was rolling the patient into the surgery room. Sometimes, he spent hours in the waiting room with the patient's family and friends for the results of the surgery. He also sat faithfully by the bedside of some patients who took more than several weeks to pass away. A few of them admitted they were afraid of dying, and they were fighting it. In cases like that, Viet tried to let the patients know that Jesus loves them, and they were going home to be with the Lord and meet their deceased loved ones. That usually calmed them down along with the help of prayers. Anointing and prayers help not only the patient but his or her family and friends as well. They give them peace and call them to entrust the whole situation to the Lord.

Viet also performed a lot of sad and tragic funerals for God's people. Some of them involved young people and tragic situations. In such cases, no human words make sense or ease the pains of the deceased's loved ones. All Viet could do was rely on the Words of God in the Bible and God's grace to bring comfort and healing to those broken souls. Only with time could those painful wounds heal.

But, amidst tears and sadness, the Lord sometimes creates humorous and memorable moments. Viet remembered one funeral that he did for an elderly woman whose casket he almost set on fire. At the end of a Christian burial service, the priest usually goes around the casket or the cremation to incense it and usher the soul of the deceased into the next life with puffs of incense. As Viet received the censor back from the Altar Server after putting some incense in it, its chains were twisted. But, he did not have time to untangle them before the song of farewell had started. When he took the first swing of the censor toward the casket, the twisted chains slipped off his fingers, and the censor flew away from him. He could feel a lump in his throat as he watched the red ball of fire fly toward the well-dressed choir standing across from the casket. He quickly grabbed the chains and tried to pull back the censor. Unfortunately, it almost landed on the casket and cremated the lady against her will. He yanked the censor back a little more and the burning charcoal landed all over the carpeted floor. The next thing Viet knew, the carpet was on fire, which could potentially burn down the whole church. Viet was petrified and embarrassed by the accident. But, his embarrassment hit a new low when the sacristan went out to the nearby Baptismal font to scoop up some holy water and sprinkle it over the burning spots on the ground. He did it slowly and deliberately for half a dozen times. Time seemed to stand still and the whole congregation held their breath as they witnessed this accident unfold before their eyes. Viet tried to break the tension with this comment, "Who could have thought that a funeral could be this fun? I almost cremated this kind, gentle grandma against her will!"

Finally, cemetery services could be full of funny moments as well. Viet remembered one summer the rain helped the mosquitoes spawn rapidly, and its population was out of control. Anyone staying outside a bit too long was bitten viciously. Viet did not know how bad the mosquitoes were in the cemetery. As he began the graveside service, he saw people slapping the mosquitoes everywhere and scratching the itchy bites on their bodies. He also watched big swarms of mosquitoes closing in on this group of funeral attendees. So, instead of having a 15-minute service, Viet cut it down to five minutes, skipped a few prayers, and told people to get out of there quickly before those vicious mosquitoes ate the group alive. Then, they all ran to their cars and drove home.

Another memorable cemetery service happened in the winter. Because of the cold and icy conditions in winter, cemetery services are usually postponed, with the deceased's family and friends waiting until spring to complete the burial. However, this funeral had its burial in the middle of winter. Viet has heard before that sometimes it gets so cold in the state of Michigan that one can toss water in the air and it will be frozen solid. He did not believe it until seeing it with his own eyes. As he sprinkled the holy water to bless the grave for this funeral on this chilly, winter day, it was so cold that his holy water made a frozen arch in midair. Everyone was amazed.

Such light and funny moments indeed helped Viet overcome the ugly effects of church politics and the uncaring attitude that he found in the world during his ministry. He also relied on God's grace and the support of family friends to keep his head high and caring spirit alive. That spirit is something he picked up during the difficult moments of his life. Thankfully, some kind and generous people showed him the loving heart of God through their caring attitude. They helped him be like Jesus in a world of indifference, envy, greed, arrogance, hatred, and anger. They called on him to live for something other than money, power, or glamor. They asked him to show the love of Jesus to others in his thoughts, dreams, and actions.

Chapter 15

Finding the Highest Purpose of Living
in the Love of God in Christ Jesus

We all have our own crosses and daily challenges. Some seem heavier than others. These crosses can be a health issue, divorce, a broken relationship, the death of a loved one, the loss of a job, or a national tragedy. We can only hope that these crosses are spread out to give us enough time and strength to handle them. Unfortunately, our crosses often come unexpectedly and at inopportune times. Sometimes, more than one of them shows up at our door. They rattle us and turn our normal life upside down. Many have been crushed by their crosses and developed all sorts of health problems—physical, emotional, psychological, and mental. In addition to these crosses, we face daily challenges such as problematic children, angry neighbors, a mean co-worker, unpaid bills, or dashed retirement plans. These daily challenges can make us worry sick and feel overwhelmed. Some try to forget these daily challenges and crosses by drinking, smoking weed, abusing drugs, seeking bodily pleasures, or gambling.

Christian believers rely on their faith for strength, courage, wisdom, guidance, and healing in dealing with their crosses and daily challenges. Their faith calls them to look up to the Cross of Jesus so that their Lord can lift them up and give them some much needed help. In fact, Jesus gave His followers this advice, "…Come to me, all you who are weary and find life burdensome, and I will refresh you. Take my yoke upon your shoulders and learn from me, for I am humble of heart. Your souls will find rest, for my yoke is easy and my burden light" (Matthew 12:28-29). Like God's people who followed Moses' advice and looked up to the bronze serpent to find miraculous healing, Christian believers have looked up to the Cross of Jesus to find strength, guidance, and much more. Viet had no doubt that the Cross of Jesus was the source of his strength and salvation. He looked up to it countless times, especially in the darkest, toughest moments of his life. The Cross of Jesus has given him reason to live and move forward each day.

Besides heavy crosses and daily challenges, we are bombarded by all sorts of temptations such as worldly possessions, power, glamor, pleasures, and so on. Politicians often tempt people with empty promises and false hope. Unfortunately, many people have fallen victim to these temptations and become their slaves. They think they have found happiness and reasons for living from these temptations. But, their lives become miserable despite everything they have in this world. Some, sadly, have even lost their lives.

Viet was allured to power and glamor as a young priest. He thought about various church positions and different graduate degrees. Thankfully, the Lord opened his eyes and gave him a conversion experience through his humble service to God's people. He was humbled and honored to bring comfort and peace to many families who lost their loved ones to death. Some cases were quite tragic and painful to the ones left behind. But, the Lord used him to touch broken souls and give them hope. After all, he knew how it felt to go through a dark night of the soul and could empathize with them.

Besides being a crying shoulder for families facing dark nights, Viet appreciated opportunities to visit hospitals, nursing homes, and especially the local home for veterans. He enjoyed listening to their stories and sharing Holy Communion and prayers with the residents of these facilities. They often felt lonely and abandoned by their families and society. Viet brought them care, comfort, compassion, joy, and the love of God. Many Viet Nam veterans have felt comfortable enough to come to Viet and opened up to him about their painful experiences related to the war. They wanted to work through some unresolved issues with Viet about the war, especially after the way they were treated by the American public when they returned home. Some made peace with God and let go of their hurt before going to meet their Creator. Viet has seen how God's love touched veterans and brought them peace and joy in their last days on earth. St. Paul realized the power of God's love and gave the following advice to the Romans, "If God is for us, who can be against us? ...What will separate us from the love of Christ? Will anguish, or distress, or persecution, or famine, or nakedness, or peril, or the sword? ...No, in all these things, we conquer overwhelmingly through Him who loved us. For

I am convinced that neither death, nor life, nor angels, nor principalities, nor present things, nor future things, nor powers, nor height, nor depth, nor any other creature will be able to separate us from the love of God in Christ Jesus our Lord" (Romans 8:31-39).

St. Paul believed that God's love for us is all we need to overcome anything in this life. It will help us overcome any anguish, distress, persecution, famine, peril, or death. Nothing in this life can separate us from the love of God in Christ Jesus. Viet found what St. Paul shared in the passage above is indeed true. It has been God's love that helps him overcome challenges in his life. It has helped him survive the fall of Saigon, life under the Communist regime, failed escapes from Viet Nam and imprisonment, the harrowing boat trip across the ocean, the refugee camp, a new life in America, seminary training, and the priestly ministry.

Surely, every human being needs love and wants to be loved. God's love gives Viet strength, courage, and resilience in dealing with his crosses and daily challenges. It provides hope, guidance, and assurance for Viet in his dark nights of the soul. He has never felt alone or feared anything in this world knowing God's love for him. When he faced danger and death, God's love helped him feel at peace and find a safe way to life. When he felt down and discouraged, God's love lifted him up and gave him reassurance that a brighter day was ahead. He might not have everything in this world or be the richest and the most powerful person, but God's love compensates for what he might lack in this life. He found God's love visible on the Cross of his Lord Jesus and looked up to it often to find help and guidance. God's love has been the air he breathed, and it has bailed him out in many tough situations.

Beside the Cross of Jesus, Viet has found God's love in his ancestral spirit and all the benefactors and friends that God has sent his way. He believed that his ancestral spirit continues to be by his side to help him and show him God's love every day. He never feels alone or threatened by any evil power. One thing he has learned to do on a regular basis is to give thanks to God for all the support from his benefactors and friends. He came to America with nothing other than God's love and a shirt on his back. Over time, with hard work and God's blessings, he has established a bright future for himself in this land of opportunities. But, he never forgot other misfortunate folks around him and had continued to help them whenever possible. He has taken his calling of service to God's people seriously and has always tried to put the welfare of others before his own. He has followed his Lord's example and listened to Jesus' teachings carefully. For the Lord said, "…The Son of Man did not come to be served, but to serve, and to give His life as a ransom for many" (Matthew 20:28). Viet believed that our world would be a better place if everyone shared the same spirit of servanthood with the Lord Jesus. There would be less fighting, greed, envy, and indifference.

Incidentally, St. Paul's passage above was exactly what Viet chose to be on the prayer card of the Laughing Jesus for his Priesthood Ordination. Most priestly candidates choose some devotional or traditional quotes for their prayer cards. Viet chose his because he had seen it work wonderfully throughout his life. If it were not for God's love, Viet would not know where he might be now. God's love has helped him endure his dark nights of the soul and overcome crosses and daily challenges throughout his life. God's love gives him joy and hope as he wakes up and moves forward each day. He does not need a politician to tell him about hope or to believe. He has everything he needs in God's love for him and has seen it clearly on the Cross of his Lord Jesus. God's love is the purpose of Viet's life; not money, or power, or glamor, or pleasures.

Viet has hoped that Christians and people of good will realize this truth and make it the focus of their lives. Once they do, they will see their lives transformed for the better. They will always have peace, joy, and hope in their hearts instead of worry, anguish, fear, and hopelessness. They will experience Heaven right here on earth and not have to wait until the next life. They will live each day for their loving God and people around them instead of themselves and their selfish needs.